Love
Acrylics

Love Acrylics

OVER 100 EXERCISES, PROJECTS AND PROMPTS FOR MAKING COOL ART!

COURTNEY BURDEN

Search Press

A QUARTO BOOK

First published in 2019 by
Search Press Ltd
Wellwood
North Farm Road
Kent TN2 3DR

ISBN:978-1-78221-726-8

10 9 8 7 6 5 4 3 2 1

Conceived, edited, and designed by
Quarto Publishing plc,
an imprint of The Quarto Group
6 Blundell Street
London N7 9BH

www.quartoknows.com
QUAR.323329

Senior editor: Kate Burkett
Senior art editor: Emma Clayton
Designer: Joanna Bettles
Photographer: Chris Burden
Art director: Jess Hibbert
Publisher: Samantha Warrington

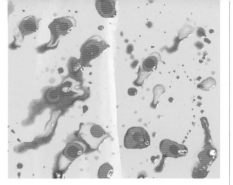

Chapter 1

Beginners begin here!   10

Chapter 2

Arty hard for 15 minutes   40

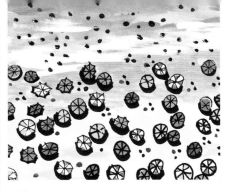

Meet Courtney

Hey there! I'm Courtney Burden, but you can call me Court. I'm so happy you're here – thank you for picking up my book!

I live in Atlanta, Georgia, with my photographer husband, Chris, and our two dachshunds, Pickle and Olive. I am an artist and educator, and the blogger behind the creative lifestyle blog My Friend Court. When I started my blog in 2013 I was a first-year teacher looking for a creative outlet outside of the classroom.

Through painting and blogging I discovered my passion for sharing my love of painting and inspiring others to pick up a paintbrush, too! I believe that we are all artists and have the power within us to create a life we love.

This book will give you a little peek into my creative process and the joy that acrylic painting brings me. My hope is that it inspires you to be more creative, colourful and whimsical every day of your life. This book isn't filled with just a bunch of rules or traditional painting techniques; instead, with each play, prompt and project, I encourage you to create freely, like you're a kid again – not focused on rules or the final outcome, but enjoying the process and soaking up the fun along the way!

This book is all about experimenting, getting used to how the paint behaves on different surfaces and what types of marks you can make – so in the plays, prompts and projects I've specified what type of paint or brush to use only if it's essential to the finished result.

Like my coined catchphrase and hashtag #iLikeToARTYhard –
let's get this (p)ARTY started!

1 Beginners begin here!

Whether you're a novice painter or a seasoned pro, this chapter will encourage you to have fun playing with your paints, showing you ways to sharpen your skills but also how to loosen up and fall in love with the painting process. It introduces you to the supplies you will be using throughout this book, as well as fun and useful painting techniques to jumpstart your creativity.

Supplies

Throughout this book, we use a variety of my favourite art supplies that go well with the acrylic medium. We will get creative with paints, oil pastels and marker pens on a lot of different surfaces – not just canvas!

Paints

Acrylic paints are my favourite paints to use for a variety of reasons, many of which we explore in this book. We will be using fluid acrylics, soft and heavy body acrylics, and acrylic gouache paints. These are all acrylic paints that vary in their consistency or fluidity. A heavy body acrylic, for example, will have a thick consistency whereas a fluid acrylic will be more like liquid.

Brushes

Paintbrushes come in three basic shapes: flat, round and filbert. I suggest having a variety of all three. Each type makes a different stroke, and varying sizes will give you more options and control over your mark's thickness.

Palette knives

Palette knives are great, both for mixing paint and as a tool to paint with. A variety of shapes and sizes will be useful, and both plastic or metal knives will work well with your paints.

Sponges

Painting sponges or traditional house-cleaning sponges are fun and useful to build texture and add dimension.

Mediums

Acrylic mediums are additives you can use with your paints to manipulate the texture or appearance, or change how the paints move and/or cling to your surface. Mediums include:

- **gesso:** prepares raw canvas and covers up mistakes
- **texture:** changes the texture or body of the paint
- **gloss:** makes your paint thin and transparent without becoming runny
- **découpage:** gives your artwork a glossy finish
- **extender:** extends the body and drying time of the paint
- **pouring medium:** helps paint pour smoothly without diluting the pigment or binding agent of the paint
- **glazing medium:** enhances the colour of your painting

Palettes

There are a variety of palette options for you to choose from. My favourite is a white butcher's tray, as it makes it easier to judge your mixes. You can always choose a traditional wooden palette and prime it with white paint. Some palettes come with lids that help prevent your paints from drying.

Surfaces

We will explore painting on a variety of surfaces – including card, mat board, canvas, rug, leather, wood and glass – throughout this book. The beauty of acrylic paint is that it can stick to nearly any surface with little preparation, additives or finishing mediums needed.

Oil pastels

Oil pastels are fun to experiment with. You can use them in an oil-water resist method (see page 21) or to draw directly onto your painted surface.

Paint marker pens

Acrylic paint marker pens are great for mark making and add an element of control that you may not achieve with your brush. They are also useful to take with you to use 'on the go'.

Tape

Masking tape is useful for creating clean edges. Washi tape can be used in your paintings to create another visual element.

Other useful tools

- straws for blowing paint across your canvas to create patterns
- props for still life shots
- photos to paint from and on

Paint palette and brush care

Acrylic paints are wonderful for novice painters in that they dry quickly and you can quickly and easily cover any mistakes. However, fast-drying paint can ruin your brushes and palettes. Proper care is essential to the longevity of your materials.

Palettes

There are a lot of palette options for you to choose from, with no option being a wrong one, but there are also things to keep in mind. Once dried, acrylics will stick to almost any surface. Choosing a palette you like using and can keep clean will make the painting process more enjoyable. A glass or metal (butcher's) palette is a non-porous surface that is easily wiped when wet and can be scraped clean. If you opt for a wooden or plastic palette, remember that once your paints have dried you will not be able to wipe it clean. Using a spray bottle to spritz your paints and keep your paint palette wet will help prevent your paints from drying quickly on your palette.

Brushes

As with your palettes, once the paint has dried on your brush's bristles there is little you can do to remove it. Paint left to dry on your brush will make it hard and ruin it. After using your paintbrush, you should immediately clean it in water. If you want to let it soak, only allow the brush's tip to be submerged in the water. Letting the brush's handle soak in water will ruin it.

At the end of each painting session, I suggest taking your brushes and massaging their bristles with washing-up liquid and running water to thoroughly clean out any paint residue.

Play Mark making

Mark making is all about creating varying types of line, pattern and texture. You can do this by using different brush sizes and brushes with different-shaped heads – flat, fan, angular or dagger.

You can also vary your marks by applying different amounts of pressure to your brush. Alternatively, you can swap your brush for a different tool altogether: experiment by applying paint with things you have around you, like forks, knives, credit cards or even rubber spatulas. Another way of varying your marks is to work with different consistencies of paint – thick or thin.

Mark making can be very structured – for example, you can create a regular pattern such as polka dots – or spontaneous and loose, where you create a different mark each time.

This is a fun exercise on its own, but discovering different marks will add dimension and texture to your paintings.

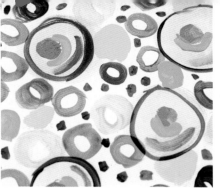

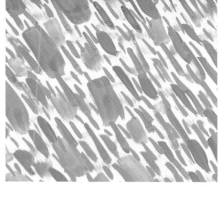

Create circles using varying sizes of brush.

Make dashes using a square-tip brush and a round-tip brush to see the difference.

Paint big and little 'X's, applying more and less pressure to create thicker and thinner lines.

Make smile shapes with a medium-size paintbrush.

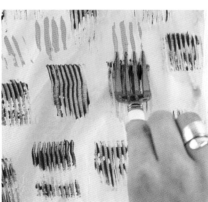

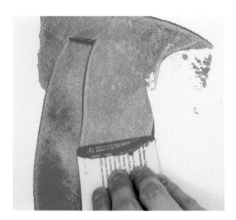

Use an old fork to create marks by pressing it into thick paint and dragging the tines downwards.

Experiment with other tools such as a spatula or a credit card to see what marks you can make.

Play Paint and create with a palette knife

Palette knives are such a great tool to include in your painting supplies and process. They can be used in a variety of techniques and help add dimension to your paintings in ways that paintbrushes can't. I typically gravitate towards using palette knives with wooden handles and metal tips, although the plastic ones work just as well. As with your brushes, clean your palette knives promptly after using to avoid a build up of paint.

Mixing Palette knives are useful for mixing paint colours on your palette, as well as for mixing acrylic mediums into the paint.

Texture Using a palette knife will naturally create a unique texture different to that of a paintbrush. With a palette knife, you can scoop big blobs of paint onto your surface, creating a raised, textured surface once the paint has dried.

Painting Using a palette knife to paint creates expressive marks, movement and a textured surface.

Scraping Experiment with making different marks and with holding the knife at different angles. Use the edge or the tip of your knife to scrape it across your surface, making unique marks.

prompt ▶ Drawing with paints

Whenever I begin an acrylic painting, I always start by lightly sketching with my brush. This is the beginning of your underpainting; however, I often find that I fall in love with the simple acrylic outline more than the final outcome.

Sketching with your brush trains your eye and hand to work together. The pressure you apply to create varied lines gives you the motor skills to control your brush, as well as setting the scene for your painting so you can begin adding layers.

Choose just a few objects and set up a simple still life to sketch with your paints. Begin with the object in front or closest to you, and paint what you see. Remember that you are not trying to paint forms, create shadows or blend with your paints; instead, just concentrate on the outline of the objects and the shapes that you see. Stick to one colour and one brush. Try it again with different objects and different brushes.

Prompt Blending acrylic paints

Blending paints is so much fun, as well as being an impressive and useful technique to have in your painting skill set. Learning to blend paints properly will help you build form and dimension in your paintings.

When you're first learning to blend, stick to one colour, blending in black or white paint. You can mix and blend different colour combinations once you have learned the colour wheel (see page 82).

Start by painting a graduation of colour, blending your paints from dark to light. (It's helpful to draw a rectangle and create a graduated scale to practise blending within.) When blending a colour with white paint, you are creating a tint. When blending a colour with black paint, you are creating a shade.

Experiment with painting different shapes, blending your paints to create form – for example, making a circle appear as a 3D sphere.

Once you're feeling confident about blending tints and shades, play around with blending your paints using only water, as well as blending with different painting mediums, such as glazing mediums or extenders.

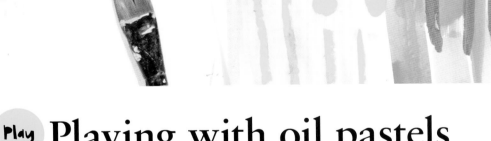

Play Playing with oil pastels

Acrylic paints are a water-based medium. Oil pastels have a non-drying binder in them, whereas acrylic paints dry quickly. The two typically work best together when you apply your acrylics first, let them dry and then draw on top of them with an oil pastel.

However, watering down your acrylics to a wash and painting on and around oil pastels creates a cool oil-resist method that is fun to play around with. Water and oil will not mix; therefore watering down your acrylics will cause them to bead up and only stick to a surface where there isn't any oil pastel.

Incorporating oil pastels into your paintings will give them an interesting dynamic. Explore this technique by making marks with your oil pastels and painting over them with acrylic washes. Leave to dry and continue experimenting.

Play Palette knife vs brush painting

Let's play with our palette knives and paintbrushes, and see which we like best! Compare and contrast the way the final outcome looks, and how the two processes differ.

Choose a simple object, like a pineapple, and paint it once with a paintbrush and again with a palette knife. Keep the colours and compositions the same, changing only your tool. You will be surprised how different the two painting experiences can be.

Pay attention to how each tool feels in your hand, how it feels when you apply paint to the surface, and how the final paintings look. Which do you prefer?

Using a paintbrush gives you more control over your tool. Draw the outline of your object and slowly build up detail and texture. Choose vibrant and contrasting colours to make your painting 'pop'!

Now it's time for the palette knife! Stick with the same colour palette and blend your paints to create the object's form. Use various sizes of knives to build up details and texture.

Play Go wild with washes

Using thin layers of acrylic paint (washes) can help you build colour and depth into your painting. There are various ways to use washes and reasons why you would want to.

Using a large brush, cover your surface or the area you want to paint using only water. Then, mix up your first colour wash by watering down the paint. Apply the wash to the wet surface and allow the water to carry the paint naturally across the surface. Try different colours by layering washes. Allow each layer to dry completely before adding another. Keep it simple, painting only swatches and brushstrokes. Try building up different colours and tones with your washes. Notice how the paint colours look different when they are layered compared with how they look when they are mixed on the palette. Explore how this can help you to create dynamic colours and shadows, and build form while you are painting.

Using acrylic washes, you can cast shadows and highlights when painting, as well as neutralize colours. For example, a bright yellow can be neutralized with a thin wash of purple paint.

Play Dry brush

Dry-brush painting is a fun and easy way to build up texture in your artwork. Dry-brush painting is exactly what it sounds like – painting with a dry paintbrush. This painting technique will give you a unique texture with a scratchy appearance, which is very different to washes or the smooth look you get when blending your paints.

The trick to achieving the dry-brush look is to keep your brushes *dry*. Do not dip them in water or apply too much paint to the tip. Use a different brush for each colour. You want your brush to be dry, but not hard: it still needs to be soft enough to absorb and pick up the paint.

Play around with different types and sizes of brushes to figure out which work best. Some brushes are naturally softer than others, so finding the perfect stiff-bristle paintbrush is key!

(Project) Blob, mark and drip: an abstract conversation

This painting project is a great lesson in going with the flow, teaching you to have a conversation with your painting and how to respond to each blob, mark and drip that is made.

YOU WILL NEED

- Acrylic paints
- Palette knife
- Two sheets of paper
- Mat or newspaper (optional)
- Brushes
- Spray bottle (optional)

1 Squirt and blob (you can use a palette knife) paint onto a piece of paper. Let the paint spread sporadically, but not too close to the edges.

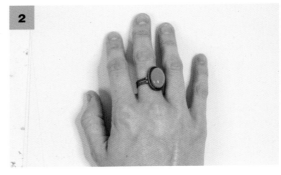

2 Place the second, clean sheet of paper on top of the painted paper, lining up the edges. Rub your hand across the surface to spread the paint. You may want to have a mat or newspaper underneath your painting to catch the overflow of paint from the edges.

3 Gently peel the pieces of paper apart and admire the abstract marks you have made.

4 Now it's time to paint what you see. Take a step back, rotate your paper different ways and decide what you will do next. Feel free to use a spray bottle to make the paint run, or mark and blob on more paint.

Your finished piece

You can paint something symmetrical or something totally abstract – there is no right or wrong way to do this.

Play Dabbing with a sponge to create texture

Sponges are an inexpensive, creative and useful tool to have when painting. They are wonderful for blending paints, as well as for creating textures. There are various types of sponges out there for you to use, so experiment with them all, including your kitchen sponge! Different sponges will be useful in different ways, creating unique textures depending on what they are made from.

1

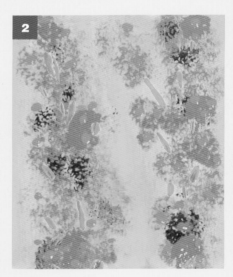

2

Play around with the different marks that each sponge can make. Try holding and turning the sponge different ways, and apply more and less pressure to figure out how to manipulate this tool in painting.

Create a painting using only sponges. Paint your background first, using a sponge to blend the colours onto the surface. Once it has dried, build up form and texture, finishing the painting off with details, using the corner of the sponge.

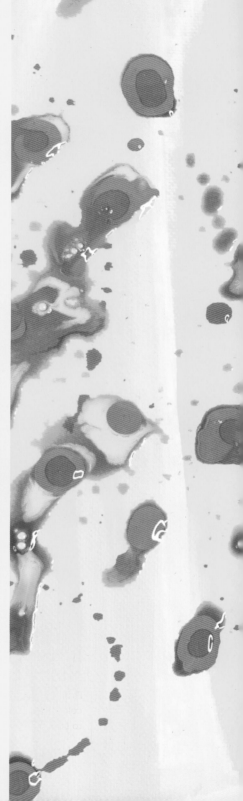

Project Fluid acrylics

Fluid acrylics are useful to have and fun to play with. With their thin consistency, they are made to flow without sacrificing the colour's saturation. They are perfect for dripping and splattering paints.

YOU WILL NEED

- Fluid acrylics
- Canvas
- Brush
- Spray bottle

Choose a few colours that will look nice and blend well together without turning into a muddy mess. Pick your base colour and paint it onto your canvas.

Squirt a different colour paint onto the canvas. Notice the difference between how the fluid acrylics flow compared to regular- or heavy-body acrylics.

Drop more paint onto your surface in a different colour, then tilt the surface up and allow the paint to stream down.

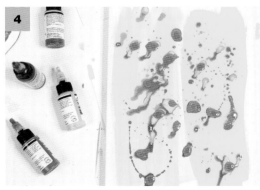

Use a spray bottle filled with water to disperse the paint, then drip another colour into it and allow it to puddle, continuing your practice of having a conversation with your painting.

Project Using acrylic paints like oil paints

One of the main reasons I love acrylic is because it can be used in so many ways – be it for watering down paints, using fluid acrylics as watercolours, or using extenders and glazing mediums as oil paints.

YOU WILL NEED

- Acrylic paints
- Canvas
- Brushes
- Glazing medium

1

Let's use our acrylic paints like oils and paint an ocean scene. Start by painting a base coat in blues and greens. Leave it to dry completely.

2

Seal off your painting with an acrylic glazing medium. Leave to dry completely.

3

Once dried, sketch out the scenery using your brush and let it dry. Mix your paints with a glaze of blue and add a top coat to your painting.

4

Continue building up layers of your oceanic scene, alternating between blue and green, then applying a thin layer of glazing medium over the top once the paint is dry.

Your finished piece

The final result is a dynamic scene composed of layers of paints.

Play # Stippling and spots

Stippling is a fun and meditative technique in which you use tiny dots to shade and create form within your painting. You can use the end of the handle of your paintbrush, the tip of a tiny brush, or brushes and tools – called dot brushes and dot tools – specifically made for dot painting.

Using a pencil, lightly sketch the outline of what you want to paint. Choose something simple that will allow you to focus on having fun with this technique. Stick to just a few colours that will help you build up form and create shadows and depth.

Start with making various sized dots for the base colour. Slowly layer in dots in different colours, building up colour and slowly covering the white of your paper with each dot you make. Squint yours eyes and take a step back from your painting, to see where you should layer in more dots. Stipple in a background with a contrasting colour to complete your painting and really make it pop!

prompt

Make a mess, experiment and create a colourful abstract painting

Combine a little bit of all the techniques you have learned up to this point to 'make a mess'. Be at peace with making a mess, experimenting and creating something unexpected.

Creating a 'messy' abstract painting in colours that you love is freeing, relaxing and an instant mood changer. Fall in love with painting the canvas and having a conversation with your soul. Let the chaos out through the marks that you make with the paintbrush.

Don't rush this painting. Take time to let layers dry and think about what you want to do next. One of the hardest parts of abstract painting is knowing when to stop. While it's more important to enjoy the process of painting, rather than the final outcome, it's awesome to create something you're proud of and want to hang up and show off.

The art of pattern painting

Creating patterns is one of my favourite things to do. Pattern painting is meditative and relaxing. The repetition puts your brain at ease and your hands to work.

Use card or an art journal to practise painting patterns. Play around with creating a simple pattern at first. Try polka dots, or something colourful and abstract. Then challenge yourself to paint a pattern with more details. When painting a detailed pattern, you want to work from broad to specific. If you like, sketch out a complex pattern with a pencil first. Paint your colours from the background to the foreground, using colours from light to dark. Lastly, paint in an outline and small details.

Play Fixing mistakes

I love acrylic paints because they are great for novices and pros alike. They are water-based, fast-drying and forgiving, allowing for quick and easy cover-ups without the muddy mess that can churn up paint with watercolours and oils.

Make it work Respond to your mistakes as if you're having a conversation with your painting. Let your mistake transform the painting into something entirely new. Try adding an outline and details to accentuate the parts of your painting that you do like.

Touch up Sometimes, fixing what you think is a mistake is as easy as waiting for your paint to dry and then touching up any mess-ups with fresh paint.

Tip

Fixing your mistakes just takes a little bit of white paint (or gesso) and time to dry.

Cover-up There are times when you will mess up so badly that it will be easier to start over than to keep trying to rework a mistake. Let your surface dry completely, then apply a coat of gesso or a few layers of white paint. Let it dry and start again!

prompt # Paint a picture of a photo you love

Painting from photographs is a common practice for many artists. Photos are great to use as references for paintings, to help bring your ideas to life without having to worry about your subject moving or the light changing.

For this project choose a photograph with a simple background. This will make it easier to focus on your subject. Use a pencil or a paintbrush to lightly sketch out your composition. Slowly build up colour and detail. Pay attention to the light source and the direction of the shadows in your photograph. Making these types of details accurate is what will help your painting look more realistic.

I chose to paint a picture of my tiny pencil collection. I've gathered these tiny pencils from students throughout the years. It was such fun painting the nubs larger than life – old pencils, usually discarded, turned into a work of art!

Project Paint a quote of inspiration

Canvases with an inspirational quote painted on them are popular in home decor. It is even better when you create the artwork yourself. Choose a quote, phrase or saying that you love and paint it!

YOU WILL NEED

- Canvas
- Acrylic paints
- Brushes
- Pencil
- Carbon paper (optional)

Paint your canvas with a base coat of colour – stick to a few colours that work well together. Build up your background with layers of colours and mark making, and leave it to dry.

Use a pencil to lightly sketch your quote on your painting. If you aren't comfortable doing this freehand, print out your quote and use carbon paper to transfer the words onto your surface.

Go over your quote with acrylic paint and touch up any parts of your background or lettering, if necessary.

2 Arty hard for 15 minutes

Gift yourself 15 minutes a day to arty hard with your paint. Every play, prompt and project in this chapter is about having fun and focusing on the process, not the outcome. Don't overthink these, just get started! The challenging part will be stopping after only 15 minutes. You'll be surprised by the masterpieces you can create in such a short amount of time!

prompt Painting and tape

Painting with tape is useful for a number of reasons. It's great for helping you achieve a clean edge around your painting, but it's also a way for you to create straight-edged designs, with the tape acting as a barrier between your surface and the paint.

You'll need to use masking tape, sticky tape or washi tape for this process.

Create an abstract design by arranging the tape at various angles on your surface. Press the tape down, leaving excess hanging off the sides to make it easier to remove.

Once you've created a design, begin painting. You can go totally abstract and include mark making and spatter painting, or you can go for something more geometric, painting each section a different colour within the designs of your tape.

Challenge yourself to create more complex tape designs, experimenting with applying this process in layers to see the different effects.

Drip, drop, spatter

Painting with acrylic paint doesn't have to be complicated. Sometimes the best abstract paintings start by simply playing with your paints. Begin with one colour and drip, drop and spatter away!

Experiment with different tools (paintbrushes, toothbrushes and so on) and add more or less water to your paint. Don't be afraid of making a mess! Acrylic paint dries fast, so give yourself some time to let the paint dry and build up the various paint layers.

Think of this exercise as being like having a conversation with your paints, responding to each drip, drop and spatter you make as it inspires you.

Shadow painting

Gather up your favourite vases, bottles and glasses to create an abstract painting of their shadows. This project works best in a dark room, early in the morning or later at night. You can use a natural light source from a window or create your own using light from an artificial source such as a lamp.

YOU WILL NEED

- Vases, bottles and glasses
- Acrylic paints
- Brushes

Use a light to create shadows on your glass objects.

Fill in the shapes of the shadows with your paint.

Tip

If all you have are clear glass bottles, fill them with water and use paint to dye it a fun colour.

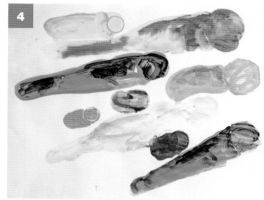

Use the painting techniques you've already learned to shade the shadows in a range of hues.

Your finished painting will reveal an interesting, elongated, exaggerated scene of the glasses.

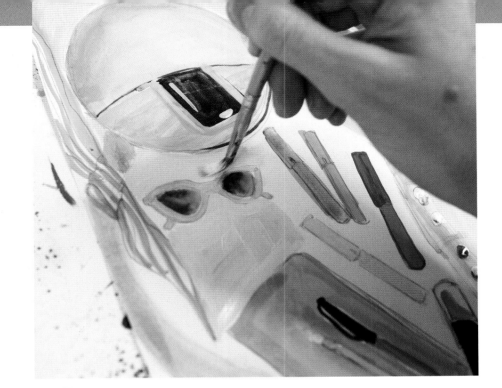

prompt In your bag

What's in your bag? In this 15-minute project, you're going to create a painting of just that! Grab your go-to everyday bag and dump out the contents. Now create a scene of what you see. What you carry around with you physically each day is a small reflection of what is important to you day in, day out.

Begin by taking no more than five minutes to sketch lightly with a pencil. Once done sketching, lighten the pencil lines with an eraser and begin to paint. Build up colour and detail slowly as you go.

Remember the things you have learned thus far and think about how you can incorporate them into this painting. Fifteen minutes isn't a lot of time, but if you focus on process, rather than outcome, working from broad to specific, you will be impressed by what you can create in such a short period of time!

▶ prompt Paint an item on your desk

Similar to the last exercise, here you are going to choose an item from your desk to paint with a limited colour palette in 15 minutes.

With your brush and a single paint colour, sketch the outline of the object. I chose to paint a vintage typewriter. It's about the size of a rectangular 23 x 30-cm (9 x 12-in) canvas. This is a great size for working quickly. I let the object fill the size of the canvas, slowly layering in colours and details.

I went with a cool colour palette, sticking to a few shades of blue. To really make my painting pop, I chose a contrasting peach colour for the background. If you have time, get a smaller brush and start adding in all the little details, like the letters on the keys. No matter how many or how few details you add, the end results are an express still life of an item you love!

Play

Art on the go

While taking your paints on the go can get messy, it's still perfectly feasible. With the right supplies and a few tricks, you can create art wherever you go.

The thought of creating art in public can be intimidating, but it's really awesome to get lost in your own world while you're out in the real world. I am always finding inspiration when I'm out and about, so keeping my art journal and a few supplies on hand helps me capture those otherwise fleeting, mundane moments that life inspires us with.

My favourite supplies for on-the-go art are my leather art journal, which is designed for mixed media and has heavy-duty pages that are perfect for painting on, acrylic paint marker pens, acrylic gouache paints and aqua brushes (with water in the handle). You can rip out a magazine page to use as a palette and simply throw it away when you're done.

Creating art on the go isn't a challenge to create anything specific, but rather to be brave, get out in the world and create something that inspires you.

Project Polka-dot pop art

Inspired by comic strips and everyday life, this form of pop art is done in flat colour and inlaid with tiny dots, depicting trite scenes from your life in a satirical manner and bringing them to life in a new way through art.

YOU WILL NEED

- Paper
- Pencil
- Acrylic paints
- Brushes

Trace around your hand with a pencil.

Add any other details you want to include in your composition, such as nail polish bottles and puddles of paint.

Paint in flat layers and leave to dry.

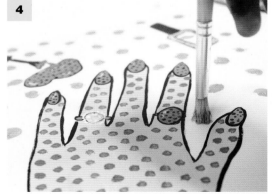

Once dry, decide what colour dots your surface needs. You want to layer the colours so that they read as one from a distance. For example, to create skin tones, layer different shades of warm colours – peach paint with red-brown dots – to 'read' as tan.

prompt ► Combine mark making

Use everything you have learned up until this point to create unique paintings and patterns with mark making. Combine layers of acrylic washes, acrylic paint marker pens and oil pastels, using dashes, dots and circles to create interesting designs.

Don't think, just create. Fill your palette with a selection of paint colours – that way, you won't have to stop.

Incorporate oil pastels and acrylic paint marker pens into your designs. Use card so that you can work quickly and freely without worrying about waste. While waiting for one painting to dry, start on another, switching back and forth between drying times.

prompt Continuous line painting

A continuous line or contour line painting is when you focus on illustrating only the outline of an object, be it a portrait of a person, pet or plant. Use your brush to create a continuous line painting of something you can observe.

Paint the outline of the object with your brush. This is different from sketching, as you want to make the line continuous, only picking up your brush to get more paint, then starting the line again where it stopped.

I really love how a simple outline painting with block colouring can turn out. Take time to decide on your colour palette, using only one colour for the continuous line. Then, if you want, choose a handful of other colours to fill in your outline. Play around with incorporating pattern and mark making to create a unique illustration. Paint the background in a solid colour, or leave it blank.

prompt ▶ Layered dashes

Sometimes the simplest things yield the coolest results. In this prompt we're going to keep it super-simple and ARTY hard with our paints!

Using a palette knife, texture medium and a variety of fun paint colours, we're going to create a confetti painting, making only dash marks on the canvas one colour at a time.

Mixing in texture medium to your paints will make them thicker and they will dry with a raised textured surface – a neat effect for a confetti painting. Apply your dash marks one colour at a time. Use a hairdryer to speed up the drying times in between layers, to avoid your colours mixing.

Create many layers of colour dashes, covering the majority of the white of the canvas. Take a step back from your painting to judge whether you have made enough dash marks.

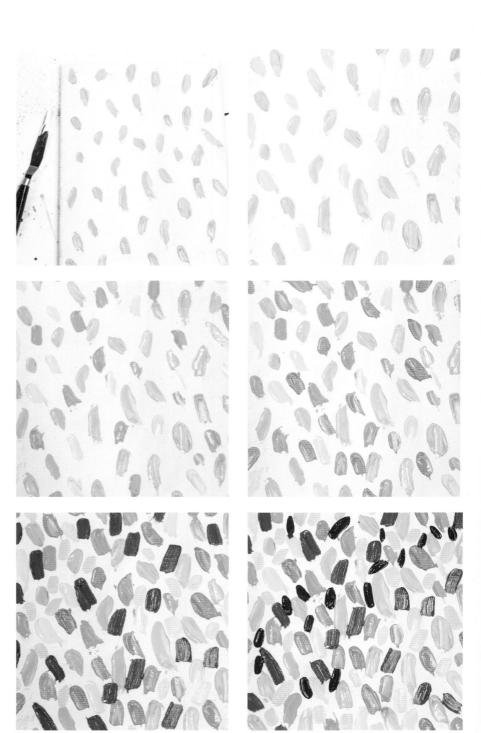

prompt ▶ Paint with your non-dominant hand

After breaking my right hand and having to rely on my left to make art, I got really good at using my non-dominant hand. The coolest part was that I learned that creating art with your non-dominant hand makes you use the other side of your brain. It helped me loosen up my painting style, while exercising a new level of concentration.

In this prompt, I want you to take 15 minutes to create a painting of a simple subject with your non-dominant hand. Don't feel embarrassed if the first outcome looks like a four-year-old did it! This is just an experiment and exercise in painting, and probably your first try. Apply all the techniques we've covered thus far. Sketch an outline of your subject in paint first, slowly building up colour, adding details and painting the background.

Do the same painting again with your dominant hand and compare the two. See which one you like the best!

Prompt Polaroid paintings

Before we posted all our favourite memories on social media, we captured them in instant snapshots. Bring this nostalgic art form back to life with your paintbrush, and paint your golden 'Insta' moments in an old-school Polaroid-esque painting.

On cut-to-size card or a small canvas, sketch a square in the top centre of your paper, leaving a thin edge around the top and sides, and a thick edge at the bottom. This is the frame for your painting. Use masking tape to achieve a straight edge.

Sketch your painting freehand, or use tracing paper to help you. Slowly build up colour and detail in your painting. You are working small, so make sure you're using the proper size brushes to help you get the detail you want.

Play Marbling paint pouring

Using fluid acrylic paints with a pouring medium will help you to create these really cool marbled paintings both quickly and easily. This play is a messy one, so lay down newspaper or plastic sheet of some sort first. You'll also need plastic cups for mixing and pouring the paint, and to help you prop up your canvas to dry.

The trick to achieving the perfect pour, and not having your paints turn into a muddy mess, is to use pouring medium. Mix one part paint to one part medium. Mix each colour with the medium in its own separate cup. Then take a fresh cup filled with white paint mixed with pouring medium and begin to pour all the colours into this one cup. You'll notice that rather than mixing together, the paints puddle into their own colours.

Pour the paint onto the surface of your canvas. Pick up your canvas and rotate and tilt it back and forth to allow the paint to flow and drip off the edges of the canvas.

Prop your canvas up on cups to dry. You'll probably need 24 hours of drying time because the paint is so thick. While this technique uses a lot of paint at once, it is a fun one to keep trying, as you'll never get the same results twice!

Play Stamping

I love stamping. It is another meditative practice, along with mark making and pattern painting. It is also an interesting technique to play around with.

You can use purchased rubber stamps or you can make your own. Use an old wine cork or carve a stamp from a potato – get creative!

Use a paintbrush to apply a thin layer of paint to the surface of your stamp. Try to avoid streaks of paint, or using too much paint.

Embrace imperfect stamping. Acrylic paints are slick and aren't traditionally used in stamping. So play around with getting the right consistency of paint on your stamp, and with the pressure you apply when stamping it onto a surface. Practise on card, using different stamps and techniques. Think about how you can incorporate stamping into your acrylic painting practice.

Project

Turn a pic upside down

Turning an image upside down to paint it is a little trick I picked up from my primary-school art teacher, and it's one that I have used ever since. It encourages you to use the part of your brain that processes visual information, and improves your focus by making your eyes and hands work together in a different way. At first, it will seem awkward, but in the end, you will be truly surprised by how well you have done.

YOU WILL NEED

- Printed picture
- Card
- Acrylic paints
- Brushes: round and flat

1 Turn your printed picture upside down. Use a round brush (size 0) and a neutral colour to sketch out the general shapes of your composition on card. I painted a semicircle and a smaller circle for the wheel.

2 Fill in your painting with shadows using a flat brush (size 3). Don't go for the black paint, but choose a brown or dark blue instead. It's easier to darken your shadows later than to lighten them back up.

3 Start working on your background next. I always work from general to specific, saving all the little and most important details until last.

4 Take the time to create texture and the tiny words in your painting: this is what is really going to make it look realistic.

Your finished piece

If you need to touch up some details once you've turned your painting around, go for it!

prompt Look, both hands!

Try painting a mirror image with both hands simultaneously. It will loosen up your painting style, engage both sides of your brain and increase your focus.

Trust me, I know this is going to feel super-weird at first – especially for your non-dominant hand. Don't worry about creating something beautiful. Remember, it's about the process, not the end result.

You may find that it takes a couple of tries to get your hands working together. I suggest using card and fluid acrylic, to enable the paint to move easily across the page.

- Canvas
- Soft body acrylic paints
- Latex gloves (optional)

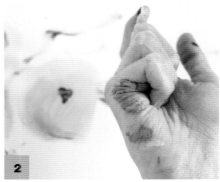

2

Use your palm and the edge of your hand to cover a larger surface area at once.

1

Using your finger, sketch the outline of a vase of flowers. You can wear a pair of latex gloves if you are worried about the paint staining your nails and hands.

3

Project Finger painting

Finger painting is not just for kids! It is very messy, but it is equally as fun. This activity involves no brushes, no sponges – just your hands and some paint! Let loose and the results will surprise you! Notice how the paint feels, how you apply it differently than with a brush and how your fingertips naturally create a unique texture.

All your fingers will be helpful in painting in the different details of the florals. Use your smallest finger to add in tiny details. Build up colour in the flowers and vase, saving little details (like the centre of the flowers) for last.

Wish I was here

When painting, I get taken into my own little world. I love this because it allows me to be anywhere I want. In this prompt, let yourself travel to a place you wish you were, whether real or make-believe. Get into the flow of painting and take a 15-minute mental holiday with your paints.

One of the happiest, most beautiful places I have ever been was in a field of wild flowers in the south of France while on my honeymoon. When they say, 'close your eyes and imagine yourself somewhere beautiful', this is what I imagine. Let your mind drift and your hands work, painting your way to paradise!

With a thin, round brush, sketch your composition using a neutral colour (I used a yellow-tan).

Working quickly, fill in the background colours. I started with the sky, mixing shades of blue and white to create the clouds. Remember, work from general to specific, saving details such as highlights for last.

I painted the sky blue, then added the clouds. I painted the grass green, then added shadows and highlights, and then, last of all, the wild flowers.

prompt ▶ **Beauty in the mundane**

I have always found beauty in the mundaneness of everyday life. Things that people often disregard, overlook or even see as a flaw hold beauty in their own right. Look around you and find something that you can breathe new life into.

Change the colours and add texture, or even a little bit of glitter, to an otherwise lacklustre snippet of everyday life. A simple crack in the concrete, the coffee-ring stains on your desk or a ladder in your tights can be the starting point for your next work of art. Find something that inspires you, use your brush to sketch what you see, then allow your imagination to run wild!

Have fun with this prompt and don't think too much about it. I keep photos on my phone of things I have snapped from everyday life that might inspire my next work of art. Start this habit and learn to find the beauty in the everyday!

prompt # Botanical motifs

There is endless inspiration to be found in nature. It is the first place I turn to when I need motivation and ideas to get going. Use your houseplants, or get outside and let nature inspire beautiful art!

Don't put pressure on yourself to create an entire work of art on canvas. Instead, keep it simple, working on card. Create little patterns and motifs on a solid white background, then switch it up and experiment with solid-coloured and abstract backgrounds, too.

You can use the colours that you see in nature, but don't let that hinder you. Feel inspired to use whichever colours inspire you most.

prompt

Facial features

Clip out facial features from photos in magazines for you to practise painting. Focusing on learning to paint one feature at a time, rather than the whole face, will allow you to gain confidence in painting portraits.

This is a simple and basic activity that I like to come back to, to sharpen my skills, refine my focus and get into my flow when painting a portrait. Doing this in an art journal is a great way to keep track of your progress.

Start with one feature, such as the eyes, then after some practice, begin to combine different features to create your own collage portrait. This should be less intimidating than trying to paint someone else's portrait.

Clip out features from a magazine and glue them to card or in your sketchbook. With your brush, begin sketching the basic shapes that you see within each feature. Eyes are football shaped, with a dark, round centre. Noses can be long and triangular or short and round, with wide, oval nostrils. As always, work from general to specific. Sketch out the shapes, add the shadows, build colour, add details and then add the highlights.

The trick to painting eyes is getting the shadows and highlights right, and using the thinnest brush you have to paint each little eyelash (I use a 000 script brush). It's the same with painting mouths, which can be extra-tricky if teeth are visible. Focus on the lips, getting the shadows and highlights right, and don't let the teeth get too dark or dirty looking.

Project Blow paint with a straw

Blow painting is so much fun and will give you a different result every time! This is a project that all my students enjoy. It forces you to loosen up, go with the flow and use your imagination. Take 15 minutes to play around and create something silly. Whenever you feel in a creative rut, try this out and remind yourself to have a little fun – that's what art is all about!

YOU WILL NEED

- Card
- Fluid acrylic paints
- Plastic paint droppers
- Brushes: round and square
- Drinking straws

1

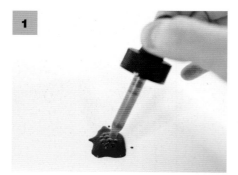

Using a dropper and fluid acrylic paints, drip paint onto your piece of card.

2

With a straw, blow the paint across the surface. Rotate the card and continue the process.

3

Take a step back, squint your eyes and figure out what you can see in your blow-paint forms. Paint the background (using a square brush) and start adding in details (I used a round paintbrush, size 00), to bring your painting to life.

Your finished piece

Turn the paint blots into monsters, sea creatures or a wacky hair-do – anything goes!

prompt # Shape face

Get creative and have fun making a painting out of only shapes. I chose to paint a shape face with blue triangle hair and round, rosy cheeks!

Start with a pencil, taking a minute or two to sketch out the arrangement of shapes on card. Draw big and lightly, so that your pencil lines will be easy to paint over. Using a pencil will allow you to rub out and redraw the shapes until you have them arranged the way you want.

Paint the background first. Try to paint carefully around the pencil lines (although you can always clean up the edges later). Before you start on the foreground (or in this case, the shapes that make up the face), think about the order in which you want to paint.

As far as colour goes, I always suggest painting the light colours first. (With the exception of highlights – those come last!) Then work from big areas to small.

I painted the background first, then the U-shaped face, neck and hair. Once the main face area was dry, I painted the round, rosy cheeks. Then I moved on to the eyes and ears, and lastly the little details, like freckles and highlights.

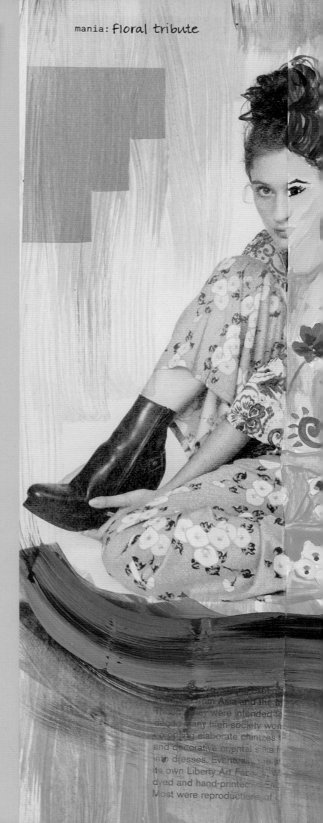

prompt Postcard

Sometimes you have to create sunshine for yourself. In this prompt I want you to design a postcard that you may never send. Think of it as a therapeutic exercise. It could be for someone you know now, someone from your past, someone you have never met but wish you could, or even for yourself.

Think about what you want to say to this person, and let that form the inspiration for the design. Take a piece of card and cut it down to 15 x 10 cm (6 x 4 in) in size. When designing the back of your postcard, remember to leave blank spaces for the writing, the address and a stamp.

I designed my postcard to remind myself that there are always sunny days ahead, even in the midst of a storm! It may be hard for you to create an intricate design when working on a surface this small, so keep it fairly simple – and remember, an abstract design can be great, too. If you want to do a more challenging design, sketch it out with a pencil first.

Project Magazine

YOU WILL NEED

- Magazine
- Scissors
- Glue
- Card
- Pencil
- Acrylic paints
- Brushes

This is a great activity for drawing and painting and, depending on the image you choose, it can be done in a couple of different ways. Select an image from an old magazine that inspires you, rip it out and glue one half of the image onto your paper. Either complete the other side of the image with what you think should be there (as I have here), or get a little weird with it and create a mirror image of the halved magazine page. This is a collaged painting, so feel free to paint the background and embellish with more details that inspire you.

1. Find an image that inspires you. Rip it out, fold it in half, cut down the fold and glue one half of the image to a piece of card. Use a pencil to sketch out the other side of the image.

2. With acrylic paints, begin to fill in the colours of your image. Work from broad to specific, adding more detail as you go.

3. Paint your background before you add in the finishing details, clean up your lines and add final embellishments.

Your finished piece

Your painting may end up looking like a bit of an abstract mess, and that's okay! This is about the experience, not the outcome.

prompt Gesture painting

Gesture painting is all about being spontaneous and not really thinking about what you're going to do next. Get yourself into the mindset of letting your body do the work and your brain take a break. Don't focus on the outcome of your painting.

Select a handful of colours and give it a go! You can start with a brush and palette, or by squirting, dripping and dropping the paint right onto the canvas. Even if your canvas is small, really put your body into flinging the paint and using your arms to make expressive brushstrokes. This is a great prompt to do when you need to let out your feelings. Let loose, have fun, and let it all out on the canvas!

The selfie

Using a variety of colours and brushes, take 15 minutes to create an expression of yourself. This could be your true self that most people don't see, or it could be the alter ego that you secretly wish you were. Express yourself! Don't think, just feel. Try to capture how you feel, not what you look like.

While most days you'll find me with a messy bun, no make-up on and in yoga leggings, on the inside I still feel like the technicolour-dream-queen-fashion-diva that I like to think I am!

In this prompt, reach right for the paint: starting with a pencil would control your expressiveness and allow you to think too much. So, start with paint and just go with what you feel. Paint the general shape of a face, then the hair. Start working on the background a bit and then jump back over, adding details to the face and hair. Allow yourself to choose colours freely and make marks haphazardly, and you will create an authentic and expressive reflection of your inner self.

Project Old painting

Breathe new life into your old, otherwise disregarded paintings. Whenever I create a painting that I don't like, rather than throw it away, I put it to one side and come back to it later to deconstruct it and make it into something new.

YOU WILL NEED

- Canvas
- Acrylic paints
- Brushes: square and round
- Scissors
- Old paper paintings
- Glue (I used a glue stick)

Using a size 9 square brush, paint the background colour. It doesn't have to be one solid colour, but I wouldn't do anything too crazy just yet. I faded my background from dark to light blue with a bit of white.

While the canvas is drying, use scissors to cut out creative, abstract shapes from old paintings. Cut freely, not thinking too much about the shapes or the outcome just yet.

Once the paint on your canvas has dried, play around with arranging the paper shapes on your canvas. Use as many or as few shapes as you want. The only goal is to end up with an interesting composition!

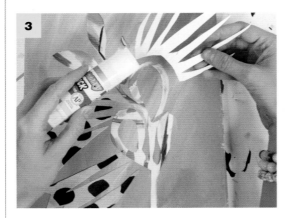

After you have glued down the shapes, use a small round brush (size 00) to add details and embellishments to make the cut-up paintings and canvas really come together.

Your finished piece

This is a technique that many artists over time have incorporated into their work. Have fun and create something unique!

Project Quick and easy abstract

This is a super-quick and easy painting that anyone can do and feel like a master artist. On the one hand, painting abstract art can seem easy – but when you're looking at a blank canvas and too many paint colour options, you can easily get overwhelmed and not know what to paint. This activity is for times like that; it is also the most common way for me to begin the background, or first layer, of my abstract paintings.

YOU WILL NEED

- Canvas
- Soft body acrylic paints
- Square brush or palette knife
- Rag

Grab your canvas and favourite tubes of paint in various colours that will look nice together. Take the tops off each tube and begin to make little polka dots all over the canvas. You don't want to squirt out globs of paint that are too big (you can always squirt out more, but you cannot put it back in!). Leave a couple of centimetres or so of space around each blob of paint. Vary the colours, taking care not to put blobs of the same colour too close together.

With a square brush or palette knife, begin to spread the dots of paint across the canvas. Keep water and a rag close by to clean your brush whenever you need to. Sometimes you will want the colours to blend together, other times not. Rotate and work the canvas all the way around. Sometimes you'll find you like your abstract painting upside down from the way you started it!

Your finished piece

Choose a handful of colours you like or go with a limited colour palette, blending with white or other neutral colours to add variety.

Project Mandala painting

Take 15 minutes to get in touch and in tune with the universe and your paints with this mandala exercise. Zone out, Zen out, and have fun letting your mind rest and your hands 'work'. Choose a colour palette that makes you happy and calm.

YOU WILL NEED

- Square canvas
- Pencil
- Soft body acrylic paints
- Sponge
- Small round brush

You can do an entire, circular mandala, but I chose to zoom in and do a quarter of the mandala. Later, I can complete it with three other square canvases the same size, repeating the original pattern three more times. Start by sketching out the mandala with a pencil. Include as many little details as you want; just keep the design radiating from the centre, repeating itself all the way around.

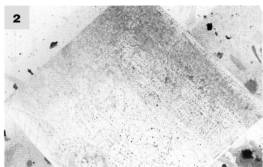

Next, choose your background colours and begin to paint (the paint will cover the pencil lines). Use different techniques in the background, but nothing that will distract from your mandala design. I used a sponge to fade the paint to a lighter shade towards the centre of the mandala. Let your background colour bleed over the edges or choose to paint them a different colour.

Once the background is dry, start to paint the thin lines of your mandala design using a small round brush (size 0). Take your time, working your way out from the centre. Keep your wrist lifted while you paint, to avoid smearing as you work your way around the design.

Using another colour (I went with a complementary colour scheme of orange and blue), add accents to your design, filling in spaces or enhancing the motifs.

Your finished piece

Mandalas are representative of one's circle of life, or how all things in the universe are connected.

3 Colour me happy

Bright colours are an instant mood booster for me, and I like to incorporate lots of colour into my paintings. Colour can be intimidating to some people, but with practice and a better understanding of the colour wheel, your confidence will grow. In this chapter we focus on exploring colour and using it in new ways, such as for creating dimension or emotion. So, grab all your favourite paint colours and let's start mixing up the rainbow!

Play Create a colour wheel

Creating your own colour wheel is the first step to understanding colour and how your paints mix together. It's a cool process to learn, and it's knowledge that will serve you well in painting, as well as in other areas of your life.

You can draw a circle and slice it into pie shapes to create a traditional-looking colour wheel, or switch it up! Just make sure you have six big spaces and six smaller spaces. I chose to paint flower shapes for my wheel.

You'll need the six big flower shapes for the primary and secondary colours. The primary colours are red, yellow and blue, and the secondary colours are green, orange and purple. You'll also need six smaller flower shapes for the tertiary colours, which are red-orange, yellow-orange, lime-green, teal, violet and magenta. If you are up for a challenge, create tints (by adding white paint) and shades (by adding black paint) of each of the colours for your wheel, too.

The complementary colours sit across from one another on the wheel and are very important for you to know. Complementary colours will help you paint dynamic paintings by building up layers of colours.

Colours across from one another on the wheel will mix to neutralize each other. For example, if the red is too bright, mix in a bit of green paint and it will dull the colour. Red and green, orange and blue, purple and yellow are complementary to one another. Keep these complementary colours in mind while you are mixing, to get the perfect hue.

Primary colours Use a pencil to lightly sketch your colour wheel. Begin with the primary colours – red, yellow and blue. These are colours that you will use straight from the tube and cannot be created by mixing. Leave a space between each of these colours. This is where you will fill in the secondary colours.

Secondary colours Secondary colours are created by mixing the primary colours together. Mixing red and blue makes purple, mixing red and yellow makes orange, and mixing yellow and blue makes green.

Tertiary colours Tertiary colours are made by mixing primary and secondary colours at a one-to-one ratio. Magenta is made by mixing equal amounts of red and purple. Create red-orange by mixing equal parts red and orange. Make yellow-orange by mixing yellow and orange equally. To make lime-green, mix yellow and green. Teal is made by mixing blue and green. Lastly, make violet by mixing blue and purple.

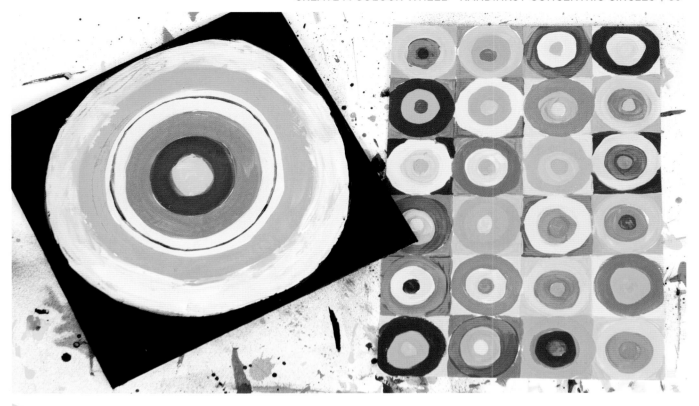

prompt Kandinksy concentric circles

Concentric circle colour studies were made famous by the artist Wassily Kandinsky, who used them as a supportive colour study to his larger works of art. Concentric circles are simply circles that share the same centre, gradually getting larger, or looking as if they are stacked on top of one another.

Like Kandinsky, I divided my paper into a grid. You can use a stencil or protractor, or work freehand, to begin drawing out the concentric circles as a guide. Work small to find a colour combo you love, and then do it again large-scale and see how it changes. I am not one for perfection, so don't stress about making the circles perfect. Painting slow with a steady hand will do the trick! Mix up enough of seven to ten different shades of colours to make sure you create enough variety.

Painting concentric circles is a meditative practice that will allow you to focus on your colour choices and painting, and also immerse you in a creative state. When Kandinsky was painting his concentric circles, he was trying to understand the relationships between each of the colours and how they interact.

Use this exercise to experiment with different colour combinations that you want to try. Don't be afraid to try unusual ones. Remember, this is an exercise to see how the colours work together. Play around with the size and thickness of your circles as well, to see how this changes the way the colours respond to each other.

I am naturally drawn to really bright colours or pastels. For this exercise I wanted to challenge myself with a new colour palette that I wouldn't normally choose. I mixed in shades of browns and greys to create muted tones of colours like pink, orange and yellow. The result reminds me of the Seventies, with its muted, rustic colours and simple design.

Play # Monochromatic still life

Painting in a monochromatic colour scheme is a great way to challenge your understanding of colour theory, mixing, and using light and shadows in your work. Typically, with my students, before we touch colour or the wheel, we work in a black-and-white scheme.

You can make a monochromatic painting with any colour from the wheel. The idea is, you choose one colour and then use that hue to mix tints and shades to create an entire painting. I like doing this with still lifes, as it allows you to focus on your painting techniques and using tints and shades properly to create your painting, rather than having to use brain power and exhaust yourself creatively trying to think of something to paint.

When setting up your still life, choose a few things that inspire you but won't be too intimidating to paint. I went with all things pink/peach, but you don't have to select objects that are the same colour. If it will make it easier for you, then sure!

Begin by sketching lightly with your pencil or paintbrush, working from general to specific. Start with your foreground, painting what is nearest to you. Add in the background, then move on to blocking in shadows, saving details and highlights till last.

You can mix up tints and shades of the hue that you chose as you work, or mix up a variety of tints and shades to use before you begin.

Play Meditative mark-making

Get into the mark-making mode! Seriously, this play is all about zoning out and playing with your paints, but not in a forceful way. Not even in a way that expresses your feelings, but rather so you can get out of your feelings and into your body, and make marks that look good.

Put two or three colours on your palette that make you happy and, most importantly, evoke a peaceful feeling. Stay away from anything too bold and bright, or colours that are contrasting in nature. I also included white paint on my palette for mixing tints of the colours I selected.

Have a few sheets of card to work on simultaneously. Begin with a light colour and simple mark-making techniques, making dots, dashes or lines to get in the flow. With another colour, start to make a different mark. With this mark, I want you to concentrate more on your body, specifically your hand, wrists or fingers. Make a mark with your brush by holding it on its side, pivoting your wrist and not moving your arm in any other way. Make a little crescent moon shape. Repeat this meditative mark-making flow over and over again. Let yourself become hyperaware of every move your hand and brush are making and how they're making it. Pay close attention to how you're dipping the brush in the paint, how you're mixing the paint, how you grip the brush, how your wrists pivot with each mark you make, how you rest your arm, how many marks you can make before your brush runs out of paint, etc.

Concentrating on these details and repeating them will not only help you get in the zone and out of your head, but it will also give you a better understanding of painting techniques.

Self-portraits

Expressing how you feel is a very therapeutic and reflective experience. Painting a self-portrait isn't always about what you look like: it can also be a way of expressing how you feel. Use this prompt to depict different feelings that you experience over time. While we may wear a mask of 'happy' every day, the way we feel may be different. Use this project as an opportunity to capture your feelings in a self-portrait.

This is a personal, reflective memoir of your feelings. Look at your reflection in the mirror while you paint, or take a picture of yourself and paint from that. Capture your feelings in your self-portraits. Notice how the shape of your face, the curve of your lips, your cheekbones and the shapes of your eyebrows change based on the way you feel. It truly is amazing to me how our feelings can apparently change the structure of our face. Some feelings will have you hardly recognizing yourself. It can be a very powerful exercise to reflect on over time.

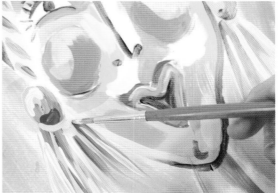

Feeling mad or angry inside? Take a look at yourself when you're feeling this way. Notice the shape of your face, how your eyebrows scrunch up, and the way your lips become pursed into a scowl. Paint with colours that evoke an angry, frustrated feeling. Using reds, oranges and dark colours will express those passionate feelings in your painting.

If you're happy and you know it, show it! Paint the roundness of your cheeks and the fullness of your smile. Use colours that make you feel good and happy inside. Accessorize yourself with your favourite items and paint the background in your favourite colour. Do your best to express the happiness you feel in this self-portrait.

Sad times Some days are filled with doom and gloom and, no matter how hard you try, this is how you feel. Embrace it and express it. Take a good hard look at yourself (cry if you need to and use those tears for paint water) and express how you feel. Not every day is going to be all rainbows and butterflies, and that's okay. Record those days, reflect on them, and move on. Later, you can look back and see how you have grown.

Happy medium Life isn't always an up-and-down rollercoaster of feelings. Some days are just 'blah'. Being content – bored but happy – is just fine, and deserves to be noted just as much as any other self-reflected experience you have. Capture this feeling using muted hues and soft features.

Project Underpainting plants

YOU WILL NEED

- Canvas
- Acrylic paints
- Brushes

Underpaintings are how you create dynamic paintings that seemingly hop off the canvas. The techniques makes paintings look realistic, and show advanced skill and an understanding of the application of paint.

The initial underpainting can be done in any one colour, but a colour that shows a wide range of tonal values is best. You also need to think about whether you want the underpainting to be in the same hue family as the final layer of colour or if you want it to contrast with or complement the final outcome.

Start your underpainting by sketching lightly with a round brush using a neutral colour. I'm using yellow ochre paint for this one, to bring out the greens at the end. Sketch out the shape of your plant and map out the darks and shadows of the composition.

When creating an underpainting, you want to use your paints to build up undertones, by creating layers of paint. An undertone is an underlying colour that reflects in the hue. There are three general types of undertones: a cool colour, a warm colour and a neutral colour. In this example, I am going with a warm undertone, layering the yellow ochre paint with a magenta, which will then be covered with deep blues and greens.

Using undertones is a great way to build up details and shadows in your painting. Think about the wheel, complementary colours and how you can use layers of colours to create a dynamic painting, as opposed to only painting with flat colour (paint straight from the tube). Underpainting helps to create more depth in the final painting. You can see the pale yellow, deep reds and bright turquoise peeping through in the finished piece.

Complementary colours at work

Put the complementary colours to test in this prompt. Choose an object that will be simple enough for you to paint and a complementary colour combo that you want to paint with. I used an example of three complementary colour combinations, but you can choose any two colours that are across from one another on the wheel.

I love plants and wanted to paint *Monstera* leaves for this prompt. You can do something as simple as a heart or flower, though. This is just practice to get you accustomed to using complementary colours to create a dynamic range in tones while painting.

Too often, artists get into the habit of using black paint to create shadows and a range in tones, whereas using a complementary colour to create a tonal shadow will actually create a more realistic effect.

Start by sketching out the shape of your object. Paint in the background first, adding in different tints and shades of brushstrokes in one hue. Fill in the shape of your object in the complementary hue to the background colour, using the two colours to create shadows, and add white to your hue for the highlights.

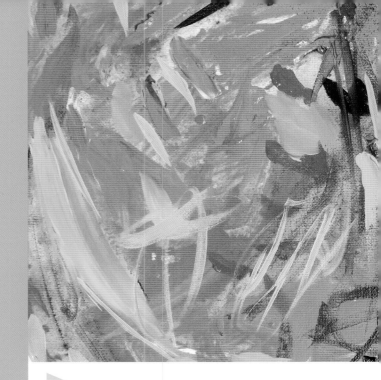

De-stress

Feeling stressed? Beat the canvas with your brushes. Seriously, let it all out on the canvas: don't think, just paint. Feel like making a mess and mixing all the ugly colours? Cool, do it! Want to splatter the paint or use your fingers? Anything goes! This prompt is for letting out those built-up frustrations and creating something expressive and potentially ugly, because life isn't always perfect and pretty.

Start with a couple of colours that reflect how you're feeling right now. This could be bold, bright, passionate colours like red or orange, or it could be deep and dark hues, such as black, blue and magenta – whatever suits your mood.

Start by spreading paint out on your background, building up with brushstrokes, splatters and fits of frustration. Let your emotional energy come out on the canvas. Don't worry about letting the layers dry: just make the mess, have fun, feel good. Focus on the process of painting rather than the outcome.

Project # Portrait painting

Painting portraits doesn't have to be scary or hard. With a few tricks and some practice, you'll be painting portraits you love. Start with something less intimidating than a person, like a plant or a pet.

YOU WILL NEED

- Masking tape
- Card
- Transfer paper
- Photograph of a subject you want to paint
- Pencil
- Acrylic paints
- Two brushes: one large and one fine

Tape down the edges of your card. Place the transfer paper face down over the card, and your photograph on top of that. Begin to trace the defining areas of the photograph using a pencil.

Once you have finished tracing, remove the photo. Choose one neutral colour and begin blocking out areas with the larger brush, working with fairly thick but fluid paint and referring back to your photo.

Choose a darker colour to add in the shadows and details.

Now use the thinner brush to add in thin layers of different colours and the defining details, such as whiskers, eyelashes and extra white highlights.

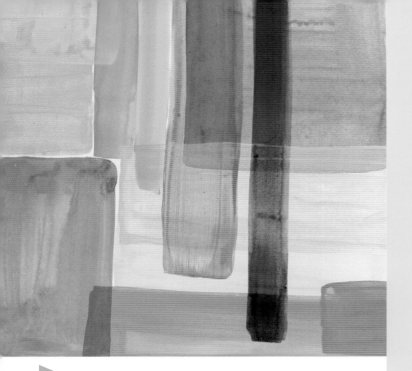

Project Painting with yarn

Abstract painting is a fun and freeing experience once you get started, but sometimes the fear of a blank page takes over. Starting your painting spontaneously, with a bit of yarn and paint, will help you to loosen up and push through that fear, to help you create something beautiful and unique.

Prompt Block colours

Using block colour is a great way to create an interesting yet simple composition. Layering colours with transparent fluid acrylics creates interesting colour changes. To avoid paint colours mixing, allow drying time between the layers, or speed up the drying time with a hairdryer.

Work on multiple sheets of card at a time, painting blocks of colours in different sections. Having a couple of paintings going at once will help with work flow while you wait for areas of paint to dry, and it will also allow you to experiment with different compositions.

Use this prompt as another way of learning how to use colours in your other paintings. Pay attention to what colours are made when you layer two together. Notice how this exercise aligns with the theory you learned from painting the colour wheel.

Challenge yourself to fill the paper completely, covering up all the white space. Switch out the brushes that you are using. Experiment with flat, square and filbert brushes. Water down the fluid acrylics a bit to create an even more transparent layer of colour.

Your finished piece

Painting with yarn is a messy experiment that will always yield a new result. Appreciate the outcome for what it is.

YOU WILL NEED

- Yarn
- Fluid acrylic paints
- Brush
- 2 pieces of card
- Heavy book
- Newsprint or wax paper

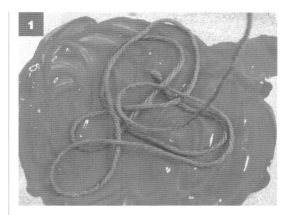

Dip yarn into fluid acrylic paint and poke it around with a brush to cover it completely: you want the yarn to be covered in paint, but not dripping. Scrape off or squeeze out any excess paint.

Place one piece of card in between the pages of a heavy book. Protect the pages with newsprint or wax paper. Pop the yarn on the card, leaving the tail hanging off the side.

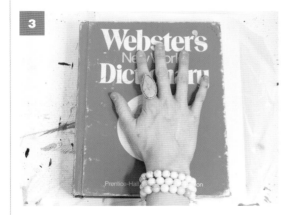

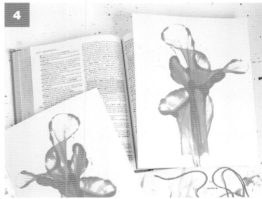

Place the other sheet of card on top of the yarn. Close the book and, with one hand, press down firmly, keeping the card safely sandwiched between the pages. With your other hand, pull the tail of the yarn.

Open the book, and gently pull apart the two sheets of card to reveal the abstract creations. If you have too much paint on your yarn when you pull the string out, it will make a paint blob. Just try it again, without dipping the yarn in the paint again, with two new sheets of card.

Paint from chaos to calm

Let this painting take you from chaos to calm! This is another technique that I turn to when I feel like I need to paint, but have no clue what I want to paint. I just let myself have fun on the canvas, using colours that inspire me in the moment. Painting is a very expressive and therapeutic experience. Painting your way through your emotions may not give you all the answers to life's problems, but it can help you find a sense of calm, no matter what chaos comes your way.

Cover a canvas with soft body acrylics, using a variety of colours that inspire you. You are creating an abstract background that represents the chaos of life. Let each little dash, dot and brushstroke on the canvas represent another hectic part of life.

YOU WILL NEED

- Canvas
- Soft body acrylic paints and fluid acrylic paints
- Brushes
- Spray bottle

Fill a spray bottle with water mixed with fluid acrylic, spray the paint onto the canvas and let it dry.

Choose a peaceful, calm colour and paint shapes on top of the abstract painting. These shapes can be arbitrary, or they can be shapes that you see in the painting.

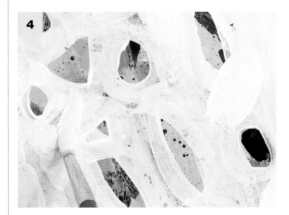

I chose an off-white fluid acrylic paint that would allow the chaotic colours underneath to peek through. Whatever colour you choose, use it to fill in the spaces all around the shapes you've painted.

Add in little details like dots and dashes to the top layer, to really make the pockets of colour pop!

Play **Art journal**

An art journal is awesome for when you're on the go, but filling in a daily journal is also great for keeping a diary of your art. It will show your progress in art and life, as well as help you to form a healthy habit of expressing yourself.

Your art journal will become a space for you to reflect, grow and blossom. Flipping through the pages of a completed art journal is like flipping through your autobiography. You will see yourself and, at the same time, your art, go through the ups and downs of dark periods and happy, more colourful times.

I often keep more than one art journal at a time, and for various reasons. I have one art journal that is for patterns, one for travelling, a refillable one and then another small one that I always keep in my bag along with a few supplies. My art journal is always just a place to have fun. I sometimes end up hating the way a page has turned out, but I never rip out the page. I either let it dry, paint it white and start again – or I just let it be. I would love it if every page of my art journal was perfect and colourful – but that's not life, or art.

Challenge yourself to create an art journal page every day for a week, and see if it is a habit you could incorporate into your daily routine. You'll be surprised by the added benefits of daily art journaling.

"nothing in nature blooms all year"

Project Peaceful painting

Something about water always brings me peace. I love being on the water, in the water and painting pictures of water! Acrylic paints, layers of colours and underpainting allow you to create a painting of a body of water that has tangible depth.

YOU WILL NEED

- Canvas
- Acrylic paints
- Brushes: round and angled

Your finished piece

I chose to paint lily pads because I thought the colours would make for a beautiful contrast against the water.

1 Use a round brush to start underpainting. Sketch the the lily pad and the flower. For the flower, paint a 'U' shape that sits on the lily pad and fill in the petals. Use an angled brush to add ripples to the water.

2 Use a dark, midnight blue to add in shadows and dark ripples in the water with the angled brush. Paint in the lily pads with pale greens and yellows.

3 With a darker shade of green, add shadows to the lily pads. Using a small round brush, add details to the petals of the flower and the surface of the pads.

prompt ▶ Colour studies

I love experimenting with new and sometimes unusual colour combinations. I am always looking for inspiration and combinations that I haven't thought of before. When you're in the middle of working, it can sometimes be hard to come up with just the right colour scheme. Keeping a colour index handy is helpful.

Using card cut down into 7.5 x 10-cm (3 x 4-in) pieces, you can create your own colour card index. On one side put swatches of paint and on the other side record the hues, or names, of the colours. Put at least two or three colours on each card, but feel free to include as many as you want.

This way, next time you go to start a painting project and are looking for colour inspiration, you can turn to your card index for ideas. To store them, punch a hole in the corner and keep them on a keyring.

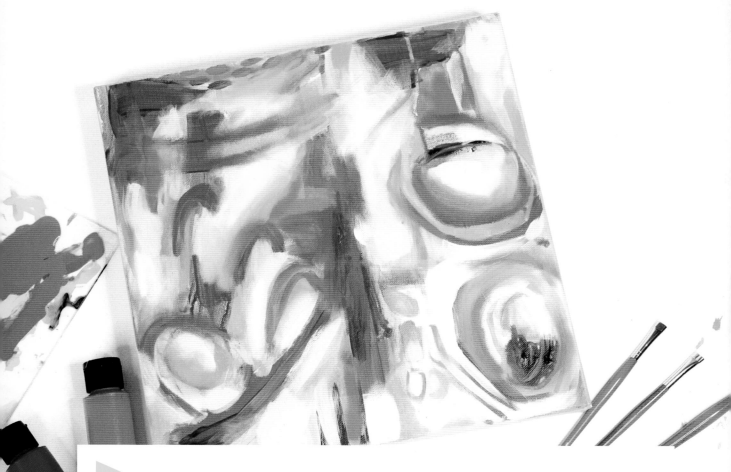

prompt ▶ Abstract warm colours

Warm colours are cosy and inviting. They remind you of things like the sun, fire, love and passion. They evoke strong emotion and represent boldness and power. Warm colours are yellows, oranges, reds, peaches and pink. In this exercise, you don't have to use all those colours; you can stick to one main hue and use the other colours to enhance with detail or mix into a different shade.

Always when you're painting, think about how you can use colour to evoke different feelings. If red is your favourite colour, then maybe a red painting would make you happy. Otherwise, if you are aiming for a happy mood in your painting, using yellows and oranges is the way to go. Pink is playful and red is passionate. A dynamic range of emotions can be expressed using only warm colours in your painting.

prompt ▶ Abstract cool colours

Cool, calm and collected: cool colours remind you of ice, water, sky and grass. Think about the cool breeze and let the outdoors inspire this palette. The cool colour family evokes the opposite emotions to those in the warm colour family. Cool colours recede, so if you paint a room in a cool colour it will feel larger and more open; a warm colour could make it feel cosy and closed in. Use cool colours to create open, airy feelings within your paintings.

Blues, greens and purples are great for expressing calm emotions and a meditative and reflective state, like the reflections in water. If you're feeling anxious and want to indulge in a bit of art therapy, squirt out different shades of blue paints onto your palette and begin to play with the paints. Don't think – just paint. Immerse yourself in the cool, calm hues, paying attention to every little detail of the painting experience, including how it looks and feels to push the paint around the palette and onto the canvas. Listen to how the brushstrokes sound as you sweep and drag them across the canvas, and the sound of the water splashing around as you clean your brush. Let all of these sensory experiences inspire your painting, and literally paint your anxiety away with cool, calming colours.

4 Texture: when life gets rough

Next to colour, texture is my favourite element in painting. It is fun, but also visually engaging. I know you're not supposed to (and I don't), but when I see a beautiful painting, one of the first things that I want to do is touch it! You see, texture and painting can play tricks on your eyes. You can create a painting that looks like it has texture but is actually smooth to the touch – and you can also create a painting that actually has texture to the touch. I am a fan of both approaches, which we cover in this chapter. We will experiment with different texture mediums and explore how to create the look of texture using only your paint and a brush.

Project # Moulding-paste cityscape

Using texture medium is the perfect way to create an impasto-style painting – one of my favourite styles, because it makes the paint look as if it is coming off the canvas, creating a 3D look that you can see and feel.

YOU WILL NEED

- Canvas
- Heavy body acrylic paints and soft body acrylic paints
- Small round brush
- Texture medium (or moulding or modelling paste)
- Palette knife

Using a small round brush, lightly sketch out a cityscape in a neutral coloured soft-body acrylic paint. Don't worry about being too precise with your sketching – this is an expressive painting.

Use your palette knife to mix texture medium into the heavy-body acrylic paint, as well as apply it to your canvas. Just as when using a paintbrush, clean the knife in between colours.

Scrape the palette knife on its side to apply wide sections of paint to the canvas, and use the tip of the knife to add in details, like the windows on buildings. Use the round brush to add in small details and make curved lines.

your
finished piece

Artists like using texture mediums, not only to create texture, but also as a way of showing their 'hand' in the work.

Abstract mountains

Nature is a continuous source of inspiration in my paintings. Sometimes I lean towards a realistic approach in painting, depicting the scenery as it appears. At other times I like to let the colours and textures be the focus of the painting.

Lightly sketch out an abstract mountain scene using a pencil or paintbrush. I painted various-sized triangles or upside-down 'V's at different angles to represent the mountains. Then I used moulding paste and blue paint mixed together for the sky. Add the moulding paste directly to the canvas for fluffy clouds, using a round paint brush.

I painted in a few triangles with just paint first. Then I used a bit of modelling paste mixed with paint to make a brushstroke texture on the mountains. Next I added sand texture medium to paint to create various types of raised layers of texture throughout the painting. I alternated colours to create a design within the mountains. I find the combination of stylized mountainscape and texture very interesting, even though it is simple to create.

Adding in a navy paint gave contrast to my otherwise pastel palette in this painting. This contrast also helped the textured parts of the painting pop out even more.

Cactus painting

Paint a simple cactus painting that looks and feels real to the touch. By adding a little sand texture medium to green paint, you will create a rough texture similar to that of a cactus. Adding texture to this painting will bring it to life in a whole new way.

Keep the cactus shape simple. Use a round brush to paint an assortment of ovals, like arms creeping up your canvas. Layer the ovals on top of each other and face them in different directions.

Then mix up a few different shades of pink and peach paint for the background. This will be a nice complementary colour to the green cactus. Use a square-tip brush to apply the pink hues in such a way that your brushstrokes are layered. This will prevent the background from looking flat and will give it a textured appearance, allowing the cactus to be the focus of the composition.

When painting the cactus, mix up multiple shades of green on your palette.

Include some yellow and peach paint for highlights as well. Begin by painting a few of the ovals a lime-green using a round brush (size 4). Then paint some ovals a lighter green and yellow. I ended up adding a tiny bit of a light minty hue to the cactus as well.

Now, add sand texture medium to one of the dark shades of green on your palette. I used my round brush to paint the sand mixture onto the canvas, but you could use a small palette knife. For the final details, with your round brush add in little pink and peach flowers to the tips of a few of the cactus arms. Then, with your smallest round brush, add in tiny dark green dots to the surface of the cactus for the sharp spines.

Your finished piece

Mix a texture medium into your paint to create the icing on the cake!

YOU WILL NEED

- Canvas
- Soft body acrylic paints and thick body acrylic paints
- Brushes: round and angled
- Palette knife
- Sand texture medium and texture medium

Project Cake

Have your cake and paint it, too! This is a painting project that my students love to do time and time again. Painting your dream cake has to be the next best thing to actually eating it. Have fun with this painting and challenge yourself in different ways. Try adding layers, different toppings and fancy designs to create a cake that truly represents your taste.

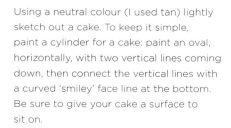

Using a neutral colour (I used tan) lightly sketch out a cake. To keep it simple, paint a cylinder for a cake: paint an oval, horizontally, with two vertical lines coming down, then connect the vertical lines with a curved 'smiley' face line at the bottom. Be sure to give your cake a surface to sit on.

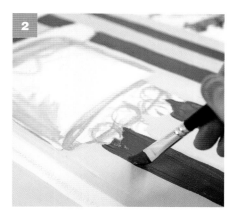

Paint the background in first. You can paint it a solid colour or add a pattern. I used my angled brush (size 5) to paint stripes.

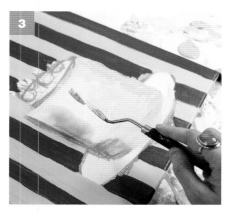

Use a palette knife to apply the frosting to the cake. Make the frosting fade from dark to light, to make the cake look round.

Mix in the sand texture medium with another colour for the top frosting. I used an off-white colour to make it look like whipped cream. After the whipped cream, I mixed in a little texture medium with red paint, and used a round brush to paint cherries on top.

For the chocolate frosting dripping down the side of the cake, squirt soft body acrylic paint right onto the canvas and tilt your painting to let it drip down the cake. Mix rainbow colours with texture medium and use a thin round brush to add the sprinkles on top.

prompt

Sunset sky: colours of the wind

From sunrise to sunset, the sky is Mother Nature's work of art. Snap a picture of a beautiful sunset and use it as inspiration for your next painting.

To paint a colourful sunset, start by mixing gel medium with warm, golden yellow paint. The gel medium will help the paint spread and move freely across the canvas. Loosely paint brushstrokes to map out the clouds and movement in the sky. If your sunset is over water, you'll want to paint the sky's reflection in the water, too.

Slowly build up colour by adding in one colour at a time. Mix in texture medium to each one of your colours to really make the brushstrokes pop out. Paint clouds by mixing light blue with texture medium, and then layering in brushstrokes of oranges, reds, pinks and purples to bring out all the colours.

I created my painting using a square-tip brush to create the soft, fluffy, wispy clouds. You could create a painting like this with a palette knife, too, and see how different it looks from one painted with brushes.

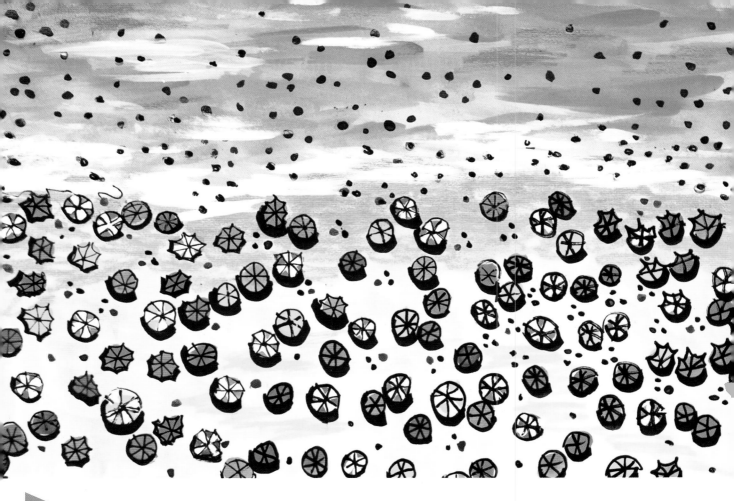

Prompt ▶ Bird's-eye view

This is an example of using paint to create the illusion of texture. You will also be creating perspective by painting from a bird's-eye view. Think about what you would see below if you were a bird flying in the sky or (less hard to imagine) what it looks like when you are in an aeroplane taking off at the airport, looking out of your window. Everything looks super-small, but the texture and colours below help you figure out what you are looking at, even though you can't see the details.

On card, start painting your landscape. Paint a simple beach scene, splitting the paper into one side beach and the other side ocean. Paint the beach side using various shades of tans, yellows and golden browns. Use a square brush to paint the sand and then a small (size 000) round brush to add little dots of sand. Use a round brush and shades of blue, turquoise and white to paint brushstrokes of waves for the ocean. Layer brushstrokes and use white paint to create the effect of ripples of water.

Add extra details to the painting, like colourful pinwheels for umbrellas, with a shadow cast to one side to show a light source. Add in little dots to represent the heads of people below on the beach. You don't want to add too many details, because from up in the sky you wouldn't really be able to see them.

▶project Create art with leftover paint

I always feel bad leaving unused paint on my palette or letting it wash down the sink. Sometimes, I even end up liking the way my paint palette looks more than I like the painting I am working on. (So much so that, in my first solo show, I covered a whole wall in old paint palettes.) The paint palette is colourful, messy and free, with a unique texture of its own. This painting will be a work in progress over time – a build-up and reflection of the colours you have been working with lately. Choose a small canvas, or even an old one you want to paint over, for this project. When you finish working on other paintings, use a palette knife to scrape the leftover paint off your palette onto the canvas.

YOU WILL NEED

- Palette knife
- Leftover paint on palette
- Canvas

Use the edge of a palette knife to scrape paint off your palette. Some of the paint may already be dried on top, but the paint underneath will be wet and easy to scrape off. Other parts of your palette's paint may be too dried to scrape off.

Don't overthink applying the paint to the canvas; just start in one corner and work your way down. If you have colours that you don't like next to each other, then simply rotate your canvas and put them in a different corner.

Experiment with rotating your knife, using the edge and both sides. Notice the texture that is being created naturally from the drying paint. Don't think too much about how or where you are putting the paint on the canvas. Let this little painting experience be freeing, and find beauty in its chaos.

Composition

Using texture is an easy way to create an interesting composition. In abstract paintings, texture can break up the composition in another way other than just using colour. Texture is also useful for creating unique details and breaking up compositions in realistic paintings.

Create a painting of overgrown vines, creeping down a stucco wall. This painting will give you opportunities to play with texture in a couple of different ways. Use a small round brush to paint vines coming down the canvas. Let the vines creep freely in their own way, branching off in different directions.

Then mix moulding paste with a peach paint for the wall colour. With a palette knife, apply the paint around the vines on the canvas. Using a palette knife and moulding paste will make it look like a stucco wall. Leave 'holes' and cracks in the walls to be filled in later. Next, mix sand texture medium with an off-white to look like crumbling plaster for a decaying wall. If you're up for a challenge, try to create a textured brick pattern underneath. Lastly, use various shades of green paint to paint the leaves on the vines.

▶ prompt Faux texture: hair-raising art

For this prompt, don't even worry about painting a face – just paint the shape of a head and neck for the hair to go on. For your hair, choose any colour you like, realistic or fun! The trick to painting hair is painting the highlights and shadows. Use a wide brush to paint in blocks of colour and a really thin round brush (size 000) to paint, seemingly, every strand of hair on top. Layering in different shades of the same hues and adding in highlights on strands of hair will make the hair look realistic.

Use a square brush to paint the shape of a face and neck, and a small round brush to start blocking in shadows in the hair. The hair underneath, near the nape of the neck, will be much darker than the hair on the top of the head. Getting little details like this right will make the hair look 3D.

Slowly fill in the hair using a small round brush (size 000) and various shades of the same hue, saving the highlights till last. Hold your brush upright, using the tip to make the thinnest lines you can.

This is an example of using paints without any texture medium to create the illusion of texture. Hair is one of my favourite things to paint; it is an almost meditative process. Learning to paint hair can be kind of tricky, but with patience and practice it will get much easier.

Project # Abstract landscape

Landscape painting goes back thousands of years and is represented in various ways in cultures across the world. Traditionally, landscape paintings include the sky, a horizon line and landforms or elements of some kind.

YOU WILL NEED

- Canvas
- Soft body acrylic paints
- Small round brush
- Palette knife

Using a small round brush and a neutral colour, begin underpainting a horizon line. Place a vanishing point on the horizon line and paint a stream from it that becomes wider at the bottom of the canvas.

Spend time blocking out the elements of your painting and working on ideas in the underpainting phase. Getting details and perspectives right at this stage will save you trouble before you add colour.

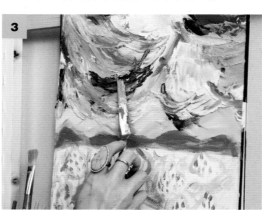

Once you have finished with your underpainting it is time to start layering on the colour. As always, I recommend working from light to dark, building up colour and form slowly with a palette knife.

Add fun details and embellish your brushstrokes to create depth and movement; I added dashes and zigzags in the mountains. Take time to step back and see where you can make final tweaks. When you have been working close up to something for a long time, it is going to look different from further away.

Incorporating elements such as the sun peeking through the clouds into your landscape painting will really bring it to life.

▶ ~prompt~ Pine cone study

Pine cones are plentiful where I am from and useful in all kinds of ways! Between filling glass bowls with them as decorations in the autumn and using them for craft projects in my classroom with students, I have spent my fair share of time looking at pine cones. They are interesting little nuggets from nature that come in all shapes and sizes.

Go outside and gather up some pine cones for this prompt. We will be studying the cones' shape, size, and texture. This is just a study, so do not put pressure on yourself to get it absolutely perfect. This exercie will help you improve your skill at painting what you see, as well as practising with your tools and mediums.

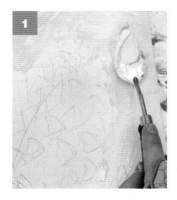

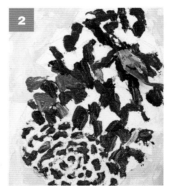

1 Begin with your pencil, lightly sketching the overall shape of the pine cone. I painted the cone lying on its side, but it's always a good idea to pick it up and examine it from all angles. Paint your background first: decide if you want it to be textured or flat. I mixed a soft pinkish-purple colour with texture medium to give the background a little lift.

2 You can use brown paint straight from the tube, but the chances are it won't be the exact shade you need. Remember what you learned in the colour chapter: mix complementary colours together to neutralize one another. Try mixing red and green paint, orange and blue, or yellow and purple.

3 A small round brush will be most useful for painting all the pine cone's crevices; it's great for adding details and highlights, too.

4 Use moulding paste and a variety of texture mediums to bring the pine cone to life. I added sand texture to the very tips of the pine cone and used moulding paste on the rest.

5 If you're up for a challenge, try doing this multiple times, painting the pine cone from different points of view.

Play Tissue paper

Acrylic paints are great for mixed media projects. One super-simple technique that I love to play around with is painting with tissue paper. You aren't actually painting with the paper, but using it to add colour to your canvas by laying down pieces of it with clear gel medium.

You can use other paint colours besides just black, but I suggest starting with black paint and a simple design to get familiar with the technique. Alternate between painting and applying the colourful tissue paper. Just make sure you allow each layer to dry completely before you move on to the next.

The tissue paper is so thin and already a bit see-through, so when you apply it to the canvas with a clear gel medium the paper becomes translucent, allowing your design to pop through. You can layer the tissue paper to create new colours, or wrinkle it up and then apply it to your surface to create a unique texture. Note how the colour from the tissue paper bleeds a bit and how that changes your painting.

prompt Movement across the canvas

Each time I break out my acrylic paints it's like I am having my own little art party, to which all my favourite 'friends' (ahem, paints) are invited! I like to crank up my music and bust out my paints and brushes to let them dance together across the canvas. The most interesting abstract paintings are the ones that keep your eye moving around the canvas – not letting the eye rest, but leading it to the next interesting part of the painting.

Movement is created in painting by using expressive lines and composition to create a flow. I like to mix in texture medium to exaggerate brushstrokes, allowing the eye to see the raised texture of each stroke. The eye is naturally drawn to contrasting textures and colours. Using a mixture of smooth and raised textures will make it seem as if the bold, raised parts of the painting are jumping out, while the darker, smoother areas are falling back in space.

Whether you are working on an abstract painting or a realistic one, creating movement in your painting is important. Your goal as an artist should be to get the viewer to spend as much time as possible looking at your painting. Make sure the movement you create keeps their eye on the canvas, rather than leading it away.

prompt Seasonal colours of the wind

Nature is always a huge inspiration for me when creating art. Many people change up the decor around their house to reflect the current season, and I find this also happens with my art. In the spring and summer, I am always drawn to bolder, brighter and more playful colours; when autumn rolls in, my palette is filled with warm oranges and yellows, and by winter time I have moved on to icy, cool tones.

Using the four seasons as your inspiration, create an abstract quadtych (four-panel) painting. Using four small canvases, create a display of four paintings to represent the changing colours of the seasons. Use texture medium and other techniques practised in the previous activities to create a flow of colours in an interesting composition that leads the eye around all four canvases.

Fruity feels

I love how fruit comes in so many different shapes, sizes, colours and textures. While some fruits have interesting textures on their outside (like strawberries), I find that most fruits look even more interesting when you cut them open and take a look inside. Some fruits appear translucent on the inside, allowing you to see all the different veins, seeds and pith the fruit contains.

Try painting a piece of fruit larger than life, capturing all its little details and textures. Use texture mediums and acrylic gels to give your fruit painting a realistic look and feel. Start with an underpainting to sketch out the fruit's shape and general details. I chose to paint a tangerine cut in half, with segments of it lying around. I wanted to capture the juicy texture of the inside of the tangerine, as well as the contrasting rough and pitted texture of the outside rind.

Take your time building up the texture and details. Get close and really examine the fruit. Adding in small details, like little veins and the gradation of colours on the rind, will make the painting look realistic. I mixed in coarse sand texture medium with my paint to create the rough, bumpy texture of the rind, and gel mediums and extenders to create a juicy glow on the inside of the fruit. I mixed moulding paste with paint to create the texture of the veins, seeds and pith.

Magazine texture

Prompt

The best way to get really good at incorporating texture and texture mediums into your paintings is the old-fashioned way… practice, practice, practice! Just as a musician will practise the same basic chords to warm up, or an athlete will do drills before a big game, so even highly skilled artists need to practise their craft at the most basic level to keep those skills sharp and refined. 'Practice makes perfect'… or, at least, better!

There are textures all around from which you can draw inspiration. When I am out and about, and come across an interesting texture, I use my phone to snap a quick picture of it to use as reference later. Another option is to flip through an old magazine and cut out interesting and inspiring textures that you would like to try to recreate.

I found the waffle-print texture on this white slipper in a magazine and thought it would make for a fun challenge. Painting a white texture is extra hard, as there isn't much deviation in colour. Using different shades of white and grey, along with texture medium, I was able to recreate the up-close waffle texture of the slipper. I used a thick-edged canvas to add a dramatic effect and allowed the texture to spill over the sides of the canvas.

To create the waffle texture of this white slipper, I applied acrylic moulding paste directly to the canvas using a palette knife. The edge of the palette knife was helpful in creating straight lines, while the tip of the knife was good for mixing and building up the texture.

I used a 5-cm (2-in) thick canvas so that the pattern could repeat on the edge, allowing extra drying time for the thick acrylic medium before I started painting on top of it. I mixed up a little bit of grey with shades of off-white paint to create variation in the tone of white on the slipper. I used a medium square brush to lightly brush the paint on. Mixing in a little bit of vintage-effect medium creates a dull matt effect; if you're painting a texture that has a sheen to it, try mixing in a gloss medium instead.

Play Rag and sponge moon painting

I see the moon and the moon sees me! Create a super-simple moon painting with lots of texture in 30 minutes or less. Using a few shades of grey paint, a rag, a sponge and a splattering technique, create a realistic 3D moon painting.

Find a round object, such as a bowl, small plate or CD that you can use to draw around. Using a pencil, draw the moon lightly in the centre of a square canvas. With a rag (you can use an old cotton T-shirt or dishcloth rag), mix texture medium with a dot of black paint. (Remember, you can always mix in more to make it darker.) Use the rag in a dabbing motion to create the overall shape of the moon. Mix up various shades of grey paint to create variety in your moon. Use the sponge to create unique textures across the moon. Paint the background dark black. To create stars, use a paintbrush or a spray bottle to splatter paint across the moon and sky.

Underwater coral reef

Channel your inner mermaid or merman, building up texture and pattern to create a unique underwater scene.

YOU WILL NEED

- Canvas
- Soft body acrylic paints
- Sponge
- Brushes: thin and small round
- Moulding paste
- Sand texture

Using a sponge, paint the background of your canvas in various shades of blue and green to create dimension in the water. Use a small round paintbrush to add in the waves.

Use bright colours and a thin round brush to paint a coral reef. Add in plants and animals to depict a lively underwater scene. Do a little research if you need inspiration.

Use moulding paste and various texture mediums, combined with textured brushwork, to add details like dots and dashes. This will add movement and bring your painting to life, making it appear as though the scene is swimming off the canvas!

Your finished piece

The vibrant colours and different patterns and textures used in this scene help to create the movement of the ocean.

Play Painting without a brush

Painting without a brush can feel very scary and awkward at first, but don't let this play intimidate you.

Begin by selecting your favourite colours and squirting them directly onto the canvas. Use the palm of your hand or the edge of an old credit card to smear the paint across the surface of the canvas. If you want, allow the paint to dry in between the layers, but feel free to embrace the mess and keep going with the flow.

Use your fingertips to scoop and mix the paint together as you normally would with a brush. Have fun playing around with your paint and texture mediums, exploring new ways to make marks and create texture without using traditional painting tools. Use a sponge to create texture, a credit card to smear or a fork to scratch in a design, or spread paint on top of a stencil and then lift it off to magically reveal a pattern!

1

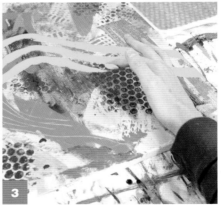

2

3

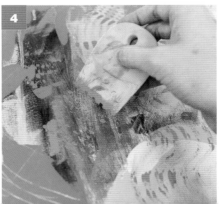

4

Play Texture triptych

Painting three canvases together and then pulling them apart for display is a cool and unique way to hang and transform your art. Lay three small canvases in a row next to each other and use masking tape to join the outside edges together, to keep them secure while you paint.

Choose three to five colours and a round brush to start building up your background. Mixing in moulding paste and texture medium will add another dimension to this triptych and keep the eye jumping from one bumpy canvas to the next. You really need to build up the layers on this one and put in lots of little details, using lines and brushstrokes that spread across or throughout all the canvases.

When you think you are about done with your triptych, pull the canvases apart and take a step back. You will probably see some areas that you want to tweak, change and add to. As always, since this is an abstract painting, rotate the triptych and figure out which way you like it best. Lastly, paint around the edges of each of the canvases to tie them all together.

your finished piece

Think of the various ways you could incorporate the crackle glaze into your paintings and have fun experimenting!

prompt # Silhouette

Remember those cute shadow silhouettes of your head you did as a child with your teacher, probably for a Mother's Day gift? Well, that is exactly what this is – with a modern twist!

With the invention of digital photography, you no longer need someone to trace your shadow. Just use a digital camera or set your phone's camera up on a tripod and timer to take a side profile picture for you. It may take a few tries to achieve the right angle, but once you get the perfect profile shot, you are ready to print your image. (Try taking the picture against a white wall or in front of a light or window to get the best contrast of your profile.)

Print the picture large enough to fill your canvas. In this case, I printed a 20 x 25-cm (8 x 10-in) picture for a 23 x 30-cm (9 x 12-in) canvas. Carefully cut out the shape of your profile and centre it on the canvas. Lightly trace the outline with a pencil, then remove it.

Now decide if you want to paint your silhouette a solid colour or fill it with a design or pattern. You can use the print you cut the shape from as a shield, to protect the silhouette from any splatters of paint. Create a unique silhouette that suits your space and personality for you to proudly display in your home.

YOU WILL NEED

- Canvas
- Pencil
- Brushes
- Crackle glaze

Project Crackle-paint snake

When a painting begins to crack, it normally means that the paint is drying too fast. When it is intentional, however, and the cracks are created by crackle glaze, it can be a cool little trick to use, creating an interesting dynamic in abstract paintings.

Sketch out the snake's shape on your canvas. Make a diamond-shaped head and a long skinny body with 'S' curves. Paint the background a solid colour that will contrast with the colours you'll use on the snake.

Now it's time to paint the snake. To get the most out of the crackle glaze, add a layer of black or darker-coloured paint, underneath whatever colour you want the snake to be on the surface.

Once the snake is dried, you are ready to add the crackle glaze on top. It will feel like a slimy gel. Do not spend a lot of time trying to even it out perfectly; it self-regulates and will level out before it starts to crack.

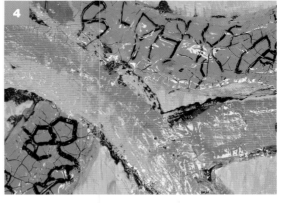

Let the crackle glaze dry for a full 24 hours. You'll notice that some of the areas crackle a lot and really show the black paint underneath, while others hardly show at all. You can go in with a thin detail brush to add in more cracks. Don't forget to add details like the eyes and slithery tongue.

Detailed still life

I used to think still lifes were boring, but now I appreciate their simple approach – you're not left with a blank canvas wondering what on earth to paint. Gather up a few of your favourite household knick-knacks and arrange them in a pretty display.

YOU WILL NEED

- Canvas
- Pencil
- Soft body acrylic paints
- Brushes
- Coarse sand texture medium and gloss medium

Begin sketching, taking the time to get your composition laid out properly and your objects drawn in proportion. It will save you time – and paint – in the long run.

I used a deep blue to underpaint the cool shadows and to block out darker areas of colour. Painting in one tone helps you read the different shades and shadows once the painting is complete.

Mix in various texture mediums to capture the different textures of your still life. For mine, I mixed in coarse sand texture medium for the background brick and a gloss medium to capture the glare of the ceramic head on display.

Using realistic colour and texture within your paintings is something you will learn with practice. You will rarely get the perfect colour or texture right out of the tube. It is going to take knowledge and practice to achieve the effects you are going for. Over time, your skill set (and tricks) will improve.

Project # Neon sign

I can't tell you how a neon light works, or what makes its glow so mesmerizing, but I can show you how to paint your own! Practising painting light will help you to understand better how to make your artworks 'glow' – another skill to add to your repertoire.

YOU WILL NEED

- Card
- Pencil
- Black and white acrylic paints
- Brushes: round small and large
- Gel medium
- Neon paint

1

Decide what you want to paint and sketch it out very lightly on card. Then, with black paint, cover the card entirely, leaving a small, blank, white halo around your sketch.

2

Mix white paint with a little gel medium, and paint a neon haze around the inside and outside of your sketch.

3

Then, using the neon paint, create a thinner line between the neon haze and the white of the canvas. This will make your sign look as if it's glowing.

5 Painting beyond the canvas

Acrylic paints are so popular because they can be used both on and off the canvas. They are a safe, yet permanent, medium that sticks to almost any surface, allowing you to create grand works of art. Suited to crafters and fine artists alike, there aren't any hard rules on how or when to use acrylics – in my book, at least!

In this chapter, we explore the different surfaces on which you can use acrylic paints. It's time to get creative and let your imagination run wild!

Play Painting on leather

Acrylic paint and leather work really well together. I have had so much fun creating unique designs on leather with acrylic paints, making my accessories truly one of a kind! For this activity, find an old leather bag, shoe or other accessory to which you would like to add a little personal touch.

Acrylic paint is durable and leather will last a lifetime – so this is something you can rock forever! Design a bag or other leather accessory that fits your personality perfectly. Adding a pattern, abstract design or monogram initial is super-easy.

If you have never painted on leather before, keep your design simple. Practise your design on a sheet of paper first. Once you're ready, use a pencil to gently 'carve' your design outline into the leather. Your paint will cover the pencil scratches. Build up your colour, working from light to dark and from general to specific, saving the details for last.

Allow your new personalized accessory to dry overnight, and then have fun rockin' it for all the world to see!

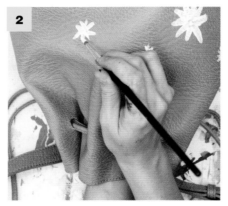

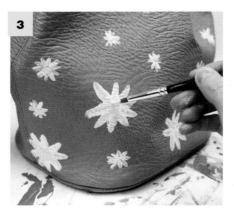

Begin with a leather accessory of any size or colour – just make sure it's not suede leather, as it will not take the paint very easily. Gently clean your accessory with a baby wipe, leather cleaner or a wet paper towel to prepare the surface for painting. Make sure the surface is completely dry before you sketch out your design. You can practise your designs on paper first, or, if you're feeling confident, start painting straightaway.

Think about the best order in which to paint your design. I added little white daisies to my bucket bag. I began by painting the white daisy shape in various sizes all the way around the bag. I wanted the placement of the flowers to look random but balanced.

Allow time in between layers for your design to dry. After the white daisies had dried, I went back and added the yellow centres with tiny black dots for detail.

Painting on photos

If you're like me and aren't great at editing your photos or adding cool Photoshop effects, try painting on them! It's a fun way to add a personal touch. I like to print my photos out in black and white and add my own colours or designs to them.

I prefer to print my photos on matt paper. Even though acrylic paint will stick just fine to glossy prints, I prefer the way the paint looks on matt. Adding coloured paint to sepia photos looks really good, too! It's a good idea to get doubles printed, just in case you mess up, but remember: acrylic paints are very forgiving. If you go wrong or don't like the colour you chose, just give it time to dry and then paint over it.

Use colour to highlight the most important or memorable parts of your photos. Your eye will be drawn to whatever you paint in colour, and this will become the focus of the photo.

Don't go crazy and paint absolutely everything as if it were a colouring book; instead, select your favourite parts of the photo and highlight those. As you can see, in one of the photographs I added daisies to my tracksuit bottoms, which were not originally there. You can add your own colours, designs or text to your photos. Use your imagination and have fun!

prompt **Rug**

Give a raggedy old doormat a second life with acrylic paint. If you can, wash and prepare the surface for painting. If the rug is new but just needs a fun new design, you are probably ready to start painting! As always, plan out your design and colour scheme ahead of time. Sketch out a little thumbnail of the design in your sketchbook and practise your process.

You can add a greeting like 'welcome' or your surname to your doormat, or just a funky design. I used washi tape to help me create an abstract design, while keeping the lines straight and the edges clean. If you want to create a repeat pattern, make a stencil out of card to ensure your design is uniform every time.

Depending on the texture of the rug that you are painting, you can add one layer of paint or many. I suggest at least two layers to make sure that your colours are vibrant. This rug will be getting a lot of foot traffic, so the extra coat of paint should help with the wear and tear of everyday use.

Project Paint a cushion

The creative in me loves to reinvent my living space constantly. However, my budget doesn't always allow this. Acrylic paint is cheap and resourceful in helping me breathe new life into furniture, objects and accessories that I already have around my house, saving my bank account but still allowing me to redecorate, on a budget!

Acrylic paints work well on a variety of fabrics. If you are using a light fabric, such as a thin cotton, I suggest using a fluid acrylic fabric paint. If it is a heavier fabric like canvas, I would use a regular acrylic body fabric paint. Acrylic paints are permanent; however, some are formulated for specific fabrics that are more difficult to paint on (like leather or velvet). Read the back of the paint tube or bottle of the paint if you are unsure.

YOU WILL NEED

- Cushion cover
- Acrylic paints
- Spray bottle
- Brushes

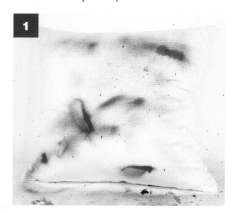

Begin by spraying your cushion cover with a light indigo-blue. Go close-up for a darker, more saturated spray; spray from further away for a lighter mist effect. If you want the paint to 'bleed', get a brush and clean water to wet an area, and then spray the paint into it. The paint will bleed as it sprays onto a wet spot on the cover.

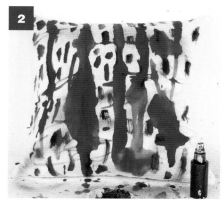

Use the paintbrushes to add brushstrokes, marks and big splatters to the surface. Clearly, I went with a random, abstract design. If you cannot remove the cushion from the cushion cover, it will be very hard to paint a geometric design on a soft, fluffy surface. Keep this in mind when deciding what to paint.

Your finished piece

Using fluid acrylics watered down a little bit in a spray bottle, I was able to create an indigo-dyed cushion effect at nearly no cost!

Prompt Statement art

Creating a statement piece of art for your walls is a cheap and easy way to add a personal touch to your space. Taking on a large canvas can be intimidating at first, but once you get started you'll find your flow and be done with your masterpiece before you know it!

The tricky part is figuring out which size canvas will be the right size. Try cutting various sizes that you think may work from a roll of craft paper or wrapping paper. Tape them up to figure out which one would work best in the space. Measure the size of the paper that works best and buy a canvas that size. When buying a canvas, you can get different heights and widths, but you can also choose the thickness of your canvas. I like using 5- or 7.5-cm (2- or 3-in) deep canvases when creating a large statement piece. It has more of a visual impact, as well as feeling a bit sturdier.

I am not a huge fan of painting a canvas to 'match' a space, so rather than thinking solely about what colours match your sofa,

draw inspiration from things that inspire you, things that you already have in your space or things that you wish you did. A place you'd like to visit, or even clothes, fashion or food that you love! I enjoy being surrounded by nature and plants and, naturally, am inspired by that in my artwork as well.

In this example, I painted an abstract version of cacti using colours that make me happy. I didn't put pressure on myself to paint a realistic cactus; instead, I had fun playing around with the shapes and textures I saw, using various brushes, textures, mediums and mark-making techniques to create this statement piece of art.

Play Skin tones

Painting the rainbow of skin tones is a bit more challenging than one would think: no one looks like the skin-tone colours straight out of the bottle. But with a little tweaking of those colours and your knowledge of the colour wheel, you'll be able to create the skin tones you want, realistic or not!

To get good at making skin tones without them turning to mud, you need to practise! Gather together your skin-tone colours – your yellows, gold, peaches, soft pinks, beige, off-white, browns and deep reds, as well as a true yellow and purple (or any other complementary colour combination – I just think these two work best for skin tones).

Play Painting on acrylic

Painting on acrylic is something that I discovered in college. I used to use scrap acrylic sheeting as my paint palette, but quickly discovered that once the paint had dried, it was stuck! That's when I had my 'aha!' moment and realized I had just discovered my new, non-conventional painting surface. And it is relatively cheap to come by at your local hardware shop.

Acrylic is obviously a much slicker surface to paint on than canvas, paper, wood or any of the other surfaces we have painted on so far. But, as I said, once dried, it isn't going anywhere. You will have to get used to the slick surface and allow longer drying times, but the end results are worth it. Experiment with painting on both sides of the acrylic to create a dynamic layered effect. Once the acrylic has dried, you can pop it into an old picture frame and it is ready to display!

Play Painting on wood

Painting on raw wood is one of my favourite things. I used to have to make my own wooden substrates, but now I can go to my local art and craft shop and find sanded-down wooden surfaces to paint on. You will still need to add a clear gesso, Mod Podge or gel-medium layer to the surface to prepare it before using your acrylic paint. Otherwise, your paint may bleed into the layers of the wood and leave weird drying effects.

Use a pencil to sketch out a design on wood. You will notice that once you have treated the wood with clear gesso, Mod Podge or gel medium, the pencil lines won't erase quite as well. Just keep this in mind and sketch lightly in the knowledge that your acrylic paint will cover them up!

Work your way around the canvas, slowly building up colour and allowing drying time in between layers if necessary. Butterflies have beautiful designs that I wanted to show off, but I knew building up the colour and getting that right was important in

helping the designs look right in the end. With my finest round brush, I added the antennae and finishing designs and details to the butterflies.

Using the natural texture and tones of the wood adds a dynamic effect to your paintings. The painting can be a part of its surface, rather than just paint covering a surface. I painted different types of butterflies, but where possible I let the colour and texture of the wood show through on the wings. I was also careful not to get acrylic paint anywhere else on the surface of the wood.

Painting on cardboard

One of my favourite and most treasured pieces of art is one that I created in school on the back of a cardboard box. Once framed, no one could even tell what it was originally created on! A great artist can use whatever tools they have to create something beautiful. If all you can afford is a handful of paint colours, a brush and some cardboard, that's honestly all you need to get started. With a knowledge of colour theory under your belt, a few colours is all you need to create the whole rainbow. Sometimes artists get caught up in having to have the right tools, or being perfect or other limiting beliefs, but just keep it simple: use what you have, apply what you know, paint what you love!

I created this simple floral painting on the back of a piece of cardboard junk mail. Using my pencil first, I very lightly and loosely sketched out a wild-flower bouquet. I really didn't spend too much time sketching, because I knew that I was going to be using my palette knife and a variety of mediums and paint once I got started.

Once you're ready to paint, keep in mind that you're painting on a surface that isn't white and may make some of the lighter or thinner paints appear duller. I used texture medium mixed in with white paint for the daisies. For the pink pom-pom flower, I used the tip of the palette knife to create texture. Be careful not to let the surface of the cardboard get too soggy, as it will rip.

To hang my painting up for display, I punched holes in the top two corners of the cardboard and threaded through a piece of leather cord.

prompt Old book

Painting in an old book is a fun and almost therapeutic experience for an artist. There is something about turning the pages of an old, discarded book into something new and beautiful – 'rewriting' the story of the book in a whole new way, and metaphorically giving yourself the chance to recreate your own story, too.

You can choose any old book you have lying around; I used an old dictionary. If your book is like mine and has really thin pages, you may want to consider gluing two pages together to create a sturdier surface on which to paint. Either way, the chances are that the pages of the book are going to be much thinner than canvas, or other papers that you are used to painting on. Avoid letting the pages of the book get too wet while you are painting: you do not want them to rip.

You can allow the words on the page to peek through, or you can cover the page entirely. Use a little gesso or white paint to prime the pages of the book before you begin to paint. Let the primer layer dry.

This step isn't 100 per cent necessary, but painting on top of bright white will really make the colours you choose pop!

Have fun, and treat this activity as an art-journaling session. Don't put pressure on yourself to create anything specific. Rather, use your favourite colours and mark-making techniques to create an abstract mini masterpiece in between the pages of an old book. Over time, challenge yourself to fill the book completely, even repainting and designing the outside cover, too!

(Project) Paint-pour platforms

These paint-pour platforms are sure to be a showstopper. The random, marbled design on each boot will guarantee that you will have a one-of-a-kind pair of boots! Paint-pours are always fun, because you never know how things are going to turn out until you're done. Trying to do paint-pours on an object that isn't flat is a little nerve-wracking, but still exciting. The hardest part about this project is trying to contain all the mess and paint dribbles.

YOU WILL NEED

- Pair of boots or shoes
- Fluid acrylic paints
- Pouring medium
- Containers to pour from

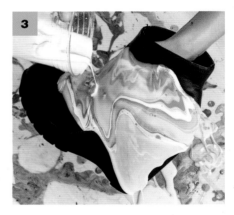

Before you start paint-pouring on your boots, clean and prime the surface and get lots of paint ready to pour. Remember, when doing a paint-pour with fluid acrylic paints, you are going to use a 1 : 1 ratio – one part paint to one part pouring medium. Mix each colour you want to use individually with the pouring medium. The pouring medium is formulated to keep the colours from mixing together or losing their vibrancy.

You can pour the colours on your boots one at a time, or pour each colour into one cup and apply them all at the same time (this is what I did). I used white paint as my base colour for pouring, so at first it looked like I was pouring a cup of white paint, as the colours sink a bit. I suggest taping off the zippers, the bottom of the boots and any other part that you don't want the paint to get on.

Start pouring on the paint at the top of the boot and let gravity do the work for you! Continue to pour the paint all the way around each boot. Wear a pair of rubber gloves if you are worried about getting the paint on your hands or arms.

Your finished piece

It will be impossible for you to get each boot to look the same. All you can do is make sure that you use the same colours for each pour.

Glossary

Acrylic A type of water-soluble paint with pigments suspended in an acrylic polymer resin binder that dries to a hard, durable, waterproof plastic film.

Acrylic gesso Preparation of acrylic polymer binder, chalk and pigment.

Additive Ingredient added to acrylic paint or medium to support a painting technique. It evaporates during the drying process and does not influence the final look of the paint.

Analogous colours Colours adjacent or next to one another on the colour wheel.

Binder A paint ingredient that holds (binds) pigments together. Also called 'vehicle'.

Bleeding Occurs when one wet colour unintentionally flows or migrates into another wet colour.

Blending Painting technique that achieves a gentle, gradual transition from one colour or value to the next.

Blocking in A first painting stage when areas of colour are put down.

Body Refers to the relative fluidity or thickness of the paint.

Body of work A collection of paintings an artist has made in a certain style, approach or technique.

Canvas 1. A textile that is stretched over a frame to make a surface to paint on. **2.** Any surface to which paint is applied: textile, wood, board. **3.** The painting as a work in progress.

Carbon paper Transfer paper.

Colour The most basic element of paint. Every colour has three characteristics: hue (name), value (tone) and chroma (saturation).

Colour temperature The warmness or coolness of a colour.

Complementary colours Two colours on opposite sides of the wheel. When placed next to each other they make each other appear brighter. When mixed together, they cancel each other out. Also called complementaries.

Composition The arrangement of all the structural elements within a painting, such as colour, patterns, shapes, lines, highlights and shadows.

Cool colours The blue/green/violet side of the colour wheel. The colours appear to recede towards the back of the picture plane. Also see *Warm colours*.

Crosshatching Shading technique built up through a series of thin parallel strokes at right angles or varying directions that create a mesh-like pattern. Also see *Hatching*.

Decoupage A finishing that can be used as both glue and varnish.

Dry-brush Painting technique using a small amount of paint on a dry brush, producing a broken, scratchy effect.

Earth colours Neutral colours such as browns, beiges, greys and ochres, or colours made by mixing complementary hues.

Extender Extends the drying time of the paint.

Filler A substance mixed with pigment to extend paint volume, used in student-quality and cheaper paints.

Flat wash Area of one even colour and value.

Focal point The main subject or element in a painting that attracts the viewer's attention.

Foreshortening A technique used in perspective to create the illusion of an object receding into the distance.

Format The shape or dimensions of a painting surface. Format or size is always indicated in height x width. Also see *Landscape format, Portrait format.*

Gesso (acrylic) Preparation of acrylic polymer binder, chalk and pigment, used as a ground.

Gesture painting Abstract painting in which paint is dribbled, splashed and smeared onto a surface.

Glaze 1. Thin transparent layer of colour applied to the surface of a painting to modify colours and/or values. **2.** An acrylic mixing medium that adds transparency and spreading ability to paints.

Gradation A painting technique that creates a gradual change from a colour or value into another colour or value in order to create forms that appear three-dimensional.

Graduated wash One colour area progressing in value from dark to light.

Grey scale Progression of tones from the lightest light to the darkest dark. Also see *Value scale.*

Ground Coating applied on a surface before paint is applied.

Hatching Shading technique built up through a series of thin parallel strokes that can be short or long, close together or further apart. Also see *Crosshatching.*

Highlights Areas that have the lightest value.

Hue 1. A specific colour. **2.** The name of a colour. **3.** Another word for 'colour'.

Kandinksy A popular Russian painter.

Landscape format A horizontal rectangle that is wider than it is tall. This format can be used for any subject matter, not just for painting landscapes. Also see *Portrait format.*

Lifting out A technique that removes paint from a painting to create highlights, usually done by brush or sponge.

Mandala Geometric pattern that represents the cosmos.

Mark making A term that describes the different lines, textures, patterns or brushstrokes in a painting.

Medium 1. (plural: mediums) A binder or vehicle for pigment; a polymer emulsion that modifies the handling properties or appearance of acrylic paint, which can also be used on its own. **2.** (plural: media) A broad term for drawing or painting material, such as oils or acrylics.

Monochrome (monochromatic) A range of tones or variations of a single colour.

Negative space Areas in a painting between, around or beyond the objects that form part of the composition.

Neutral colour Neither a warm nor cool colour. Sometimes referring to colours not included on the colour wheel and not associated with a hue, such as browns, greys, whites and blacks. Neutrals result from combining two complementary colours.

Neutral colours Colours toned down by adding white, grey or black, or by mixing them with a complementary colour.

Palette 1. Receptacles made of wood, metal, plastic or glass used by the artist for mixing paint. **2.** Figuratively, the range of colours used by the artist.

Pigment The colour element in paint. Dry, ground and powdered colour that is mixed into a medium such as acrylic polymer resin to make a chromatic paint. There are

thousands of natural and synthetic pigments available, which all behave differently.

Pop art An art movement popular in the 1950s–60s, including images from popular culture found in mundane everyday life.

Portrait format A vertical rectangle that is taller than it is wide. This format can be used for any subject matter, not just for portraits. Also see *Landscape format.*

Pouring medium An additive used as a diluting agent and binder to help paint consistency and flow across a surface.

Primary colours Yellow, red and blue – the colours that can't be made by mixing others. Also called 'primaries'.

Saturation The purity and strength of a colour. Paint as it comes from the tube is at maximum saturation; once other hues are added, saturation decreases.

Secondary colours Green, orange and violet – made by mixing two primaries.

Shade A colour with black or other dark colours mixed into it, creating a darker version.

Spattering A technique that creates random droplets of paint.

Still life A painting of primarily inanimate objects.

Stippling A technique that applies small dots of colour with the tip of a brush.

Studio The artist's workroom or workshop.

Study A practice painting made in order to capture the essence of a subject or scene, or to evaluate a composition.

Temperature Refers to the warmness or coolness of a colour.

Tertiary colours 1. The six colours between primaries and secondaries on the colour wheel: red-orange, yellow-orange, yellow-green, blue-green, blue-violet and red-violet. **2.** Brown tones (russet, citrine and olive) made by mixing all three primaries in different proportions. Also called 'intermediate colours'.

Thumbnail Small, rough sketch delineating the elements of a future painting to further develop an idea or try out different compositions.

Tint A lighter value of a colour made by adding white.

Tinting strength The degree of intensity in which a particular colour or pigment affects another one when mixed with it.

Tone The lightness or darkness of a colour, rather than actual hue. Also called 'value'.

Triptych A painting on three panels.

Underpainting The first layers of paint established in a painting, before any details are painted.

Undertone The colour seen when a paint colour is spread very thinly.

Value The lightness or darkness of a colour, rather than the actual hue.

Value scale Progression of tones from the lightest light to the darkest dark. Also see *Grey scale.*

Varnish A transparent, protective coating added to a finished, dry painting.

Veil A thin transparent layer of paint that produces a veil or fog. Useful to lighten areas or tone down colours.

Warm colours The red/orange/yellow side of the wheel. These colours appear to advance towards the foreground. Also see *Cool colours.*

Wash Thin, fluid, usually translucent coat of paint, typically over large areas. Also see *Flat wash, Graduated wash.*

Wet-in-wet Painting technique where wet paint is applied to a wet surface, so that colours can blend and mix together on the painting surface.

Wet-on-dry Painting with fresh wet paint applied onto a layer of dry paint.

Index

Illustrations are in *italic*. Projects are in **bold**.

Credits

I dedicate this book to my late grandmother, Vivian. You always encouraged my creative endeavours and my dream of writing a book. I lost you while I was creating this book, but I know you would be proud.

And to my loving husband, best friend and number one supporter, Chris. I couldn't have done this without you, and I am always thankful to have you by my side in all that I do. #Forevera BURDEN

About Court

Courtney Burden is an Atlanta-based artist and educator, and is the blogger behind the hugely popular art and lifestyle blog My Friend Court (www.myfriendcourt.com). Teaching elementary-school art for five years, as well as online painting courses, Courtney has a passion for sharing the artistic experience with others. She is inspired by colour and travel, and loves to hang out with her two dachshunds.